Notes & Apologies:

✷ We are proud to present, as a complement to this year's
special audio bonus: Believer Radio. Hosted by the issue's contributors,
these sixteen shows dive deeper into the musicians and subjects explored
in the print magazine. For more information on each episode, check
out the table of contents on page 6. And to listen to all the offerings,
please visit BFF.fm/believer. We're grateful to our partners in this sonic
extravaganza, BFF.fm (Best Frequencies Forever), a community radio
station based in San Francisco's Mission District. BFF.fm celebrated its
tenth anniversary this year, and it continues to produce exceedingly good
internet-radio programming year-round. To support its efforts, please
consider making a donation at BFF.fm/donate. Thanks for listening.

✷ This issue's cover depicts, from left to right, Vieux Farka Touré, Dolly
Parton, PJ Harvey, Jimin, Mariah Carey, Natalie Merchant, Lol Tolhurst,
and an unnamed funerary violinist.

✷ Scattered throughout this issue is a microinterview with Victor Oladipo,
conducted by Alan Chazaro. Oladipo is a shooting guard for the Houston
Rockets, a two-time NBA All-Star, a former number two overall pick, and
an accomplished musician, who recently released a new Afrobeats album,
TUNDE. Victor spoke to Alan from his home in the greater Washington,
DC, Area, right after he put his infant daughter to sleep. The interview
was slightly delayed because she didn't go down easy.

✷ Annual subscriptions to *The Believer* include four issues, one of which
might be themed (like this one, for example) and may come with a bonus
item, such as a giant poster or art object. View our subscription deals at
thebeliever.net/subscribe.

✷ The incidental illustrations in this issue, of notable musicians' eyewear,
are by Yann Le Bec.

DEAR THE BELIEVER

849 VALENCIA STREET, SAN FRANCISCO, CA 94110

letters@thebeliever.net

Dear Believer,

As an Indiana native and *Garfield* super-fan, I was so excited to see you cover the comic strip's history in issue 143! There are some things in the feature ("Lasagna Nation," Fall 2023) that even *I* didn't know!

One particular thing that caught my attention was the mystery surrounding "the hundreds of Garf phones that have been washing up on a French beach for three decades." I had to know more! So I did some digging, and I wanted to share my findings with you.

In the 1980s, Brittany was heavily afflicted by a barrage of thousands of bright orange Garfield phones that appeared on its beaches, seemingly with no end. This puzzled tourists, locals, and environmentalists for decades—that is, until 2019, when local farmer René Morvan provided a breakthrough in the case. After seeing a report about the issue, Morvan came forward to say that, in the '80s, he and his brother had discovered a metal shipping container filled to the brim with Garfield phones hidden away in an undersea cave. He brought a group of environmentalists over to the cave, but there was almost nothing left: the thousands of plastic Garfield phones had entered the ocean.

While this letter started out as a platform to express my love for the fat, lasagna-eating cat, I think it must end as a plea to use less plastic, which pollutes our oceans. According to the Natural History Museum in London, between 4.8 million and 12.7 million tons of plastic enter the ocean each year. Yikes! As much as we all love him, please do not let Garfield destroy the world.

All my best,
Delilah Crawford
New Albany, IN

Dear Believer,

I thought Anika Banister's essay on *Garfield* was excellent. It reminded me of the brief and tragic life of Garfield-EATS, a delivery-based restaurant located down the street from my apartment in Toronto. Jim Davis himself promoted the business as "enter-gaging" (a portmanteau that speaks to its ordering app, which played old episodes of *Garfield and Friends*) in a terrifyingly staged YouTube video, before it shuttered on Christmas Eve of 2021. It is survived only by a few think pieces and social media accounts, kept active with wistful tweets ("Once upon a time, family mattered...") and links to Medium articles ("Entrepreneurship is not black or white—it is also orange") penned by one passionate restaurateur.

Anyway, that's all I've got for you. Thanks to Anika for the article.

Yours,
Claire A.
Toronto, Canada

Dear Believer,

I just finished the profile on John Wilson ("How to Walk Around New York," Summer 2023), and the phrase "the real unreality of New York City" got me thinking about my time in New York. I moved there from the West Coast right around the time I started to read and subscribe to *The Believer*. I was in my twenties, and I was taking off for the big city, with a girl, for theater and for adventure away from family and the "old me." Reading your magazine was part of that time in my life. I was curious and trying to find myself by plunging into the world away from home. You were covering art exhibitions in New York featuring works that highlighted stories of "the disappeared in South America" and the post-9/11 surveillance world. Because of your publication, I not only had things to do on the weekend and interesting subjects to bring up at parties; I was also seeing the world.

Now I'm married and live in New Jersey, and although the city is a half mile across the Hudson River, New York has never felt so far away. But despite twenty years and despite my *Believer* archive (c. 2006–2012) being donated to Housing Works Bookstore, I get to experience New York and the world through your eyes *again*, thanks to the Kickstarter campaign (I'm a backer!). And thanks to the John Wilson profile, I also get to see it through his eyes, and my wife and I have something to watch in the evenings.
David Sanchez
Edgewater, NJ

P.S. Love the games! Though the crossword puzzle is fucking hard.

3

JG: I was once scolded at a party. Somebody said something I thought was just really funny and I was like, Oh, I've got to remember this dialogue I'm hearing, and I ran over to my schoolbag to get a notebook. Somebody followed me and was like, "Put it back in the bag. Don't do it."

Compiled by Emily Lang; photo of IVE by Korea.net / Korean Culture and Information Service (Jeon Han); portraits by Kristian Hammerstad

BLVR: Nobody wants to pigeonhole themselves into a single movement. But if you had to define it, what is goth?

LT: I believe the word *goth* was originally used to describe medieval churches where the central architectural feature was the windows that would let in light. I like this origin of the word because it seems like an accurate description of what goth music is doing too. Goth music lets the light in.

PJH: Everything I come across that's new all somehow goes into the well of me. And that might turn around and come out as a piece of work at some point.

RG: Would I like some interest from the mainstream Black media? Sure, but I know I'm niche. So OK, fine. Can somebody over there pick up the damn banjo? Once Beyoncé picks up the banjo, my job is done.

Rock illustrations by Andrea Settimo

WELCOME TO BELIEVER RADIO

SIXTEEN(ISH) HOURS OF ORIGINAL RADIO PROGRAMMING, BROADCAST ON BFF.FM

produced by Claire Mullen

For this issue, we asked several of our contributors to curate hour-long DJ sets that were related, in some way, to the articles they wrote for print. All shows are available for free at BFF.fm/believer.

1. "A MAP OF THE SOUL," AKU AMMAH-TAGOE AND MIMI LOK

Two learned fans highlight the BTS songs that illustrate Jungian concepts of the self, and discuss what sets the group apart in the broader pop landscape.

2. "BACK TO BASICS," CARRIE BROWNSTEIN

Our advice columnist reminds you of the many reasons to love the electric guitar.

3. "ICEBERG HEART," GABRIEL BUMP

A selection of songs dealing with conflicted romance.

4. "NBA JAMS," ALAN CHAZARO

All the best NBA rappers in just one hour, with a few wild cards thrown in there.

5. "MUSICAL SUBSTITUTIONS," PAUL COLLINS

Can auto junkyard 8-track decks replace the orchestra in a Top 40 hit? Maybe. Can four kazoos replace a pipe organ? Maybe not.

6. "UPDATED MAILING LIST," ANAÏS DUPLAN

On the most recent wave of "intelligent dance music," in which artists of color are reworking a (historically white) category of electronica.

7. "CDMX LOVE SONGS," RICARDO FRASSO JARAMILLO

A series of love songs that feature Mexico City as a setting or muse, with a focus on recently released music by the CDMX-based experimental collective Amor Muere.

8. "MUSIC FOR DUNGEONS," STU HORVATH

Descend into the depths of dungeonsynth's thirty-year history.

9. "I BELIEVE IN YOU AND YOUR POWERPOINT," JEREMY GAUDET AND RYAN H. WALSH

Two musicians select the most lyrically creative songs they know and discuss what makes them so exceptional.

10. "LITTLE SPARROW," EMMA INGRISANI

A look at the prodigious musical talents of Dolly Parton, whose connection to rock and roll has been complex and oddly fraught.

11. "LOVE AND BASEMENTS," CASEY JARMAN

An unapologetic (OK, slightly apologetic) return to the Portland, Oregon, house show scene circa 2005–10.

12. "ABOVE AND BEYOND 10,000 MANIACS," LAUREN LEBLANC

A deep dive into the forty-year (and counting!) career, collaborations, and activism of Natalie Merchant.

13. "MBE AND ME," MELISSA LOCKER

An hour of music from artists who have been made Members of the Order of the British Empire (including PJ Harvey).

14. "BLESSED ARE THE POOR IN SPIRIT," MIKE MCGONIGAL

A celebration of street-corner evangelist recordings.

15. "DELIRIUM TIME," NIELA ORR

Looking at the different musical textures in the film Glitter and the intermingling creative sensibilities of the post-disco era.

16. "ALL THAT HAS DARK SOUNDS," LOL AND GRAY TOLHURST

A mix of goth music, tracing its origins from 1980s England to its contemporary global diaspora.

RESURRECTOR

A ROTATING GUEST COLUMN IN WHICH WRITERS REEXAMINE CRITICALLY UNACCLAIMED WORKS OF ART. IN THIS ISSUE: *GLITTER*

by Niela Orr

In 2001, ten days after the 9/11 attacks, *Glitter* premiered in theaters. In the film, Mariah Carey stars as Billie Frank, a gifted vocalist and club dancer who makes it big in early 1980s New York City, after she is discovered singing background vocals for a plastic diva. Billie and her manager, the downtown DJ who plucked her out of the club, a tortured artist and impresario named Dice (Max Beesley), gamble big on her talent. Predictably, they also fall in love. Owing to its thin plot, misplaced mood, production delays, and what Carey has characterized as extensive rewrites and meddling from producers and other bigwigs, including her ex-husband Tommy Mottola, who was then a powerful music executive, *Glitter* is considered one of the worst movies of all time. Indeed, it fails to capitalize on a tried-and-true Hollywood romantic formula. It's *A Star Is Born*, dimmed, demoted, sent straight to video; *Mahogany* unvarnished; *The Bodyguard*'s badly coordinated body double; *Sparkle* sputtered, snuffed out.

To paraphrase a line from an old Dave Chappelle skit, what can you say about *Glitter* that hasn't already been said about Cinderella's glass slipper? It is a shiny piece whose condition of being lost in the shuffle and in the unfurling of mythos—in this case, the tragedies of the 9/11 attacks, and the national storytelling associated with it—is its central symbolic feature. What can you say about the movie that hasn't already been observed about confetti splooged out of canons and trampled in Times Square? It's a fucking mess that sometimes looks great. The camerawork zips, fast-forwards, zags, whiplashes from one dead-end plot point to the next, one enervating set piece to another. Its speed is just kinetic emptiness, like the ragged, nonstop motion of an activity induced by uppers. To employ one last, ridiculously belated description of its character, *Glitter* is an upturned sugar stick, its sparkly sediment shimmering in the sun, still sticky on your hands hours—in this case *years*—later.

Somehow, American pop culture is still stuck on *Glitter*. A few years ago, the soundtrack went to number one on the iTunes charts—apparently there was a fan-driven #JusticeForGlitter social media campaign that generated renewed interest in the

Illustration by Andrea Settimo

project. The greatest irony of the movie is that it had all the makings of a fantastic pop song: it featured a phenomenal singer, and its narrative was the stuff of the great American songbook—yearning, ambition, and unrelenting love. But the soundtrack is sumptuous, and it was surprisingly successful, despite the pervading critical opinion that the album's many rap features prevented it from achieving verisimilitude to '80s dance music, and despite bearing the ignominious distinction of having been released on September 11. "Didn't Mean to Turn You On" and "Don't Stop" are both compressions of sonic "ecstasy," a term that appears throughout the album. "Loverboy," the best-selling single of 2001, which went to number two on the Billboard Hot 100, is a candy ring melting in the desert, plastic and syrup coagulating in shifting sand. Its lyrics and campy music video unintentionally jibe with the public perception of Carey's nervous breakdown, one that involved her ill-fated promo appearance on *TRL*, in which she stripped to her skivvies and delivered ice cream to the audience. ("The problem is, if you don't have ice cream in your life, sometimes you might just go a little bit crazy," Carey told a stiff and unaccommodating Carson Daly, who, doing his worst David Letterman impression, replied, "That's a metaphor for a lot more, I'm sure.") In one line from "Loverboy," Carey sings: "And when my sugar daddy / takes me for a ride / whatever way we go it's / delirium time." That last phrase, "delirium time," captures the rapturous quality of being in love, and of being overwhelmed. It sums up a dizzying period that encapsulates Carey's public mental health struggle, much of which was spurred by exhaustion and the media's relentless bullying.

The emotional dichotomy of *Glitter* and its soundtrack parallels the binary that one might find in the gender stratifications of romance films like these, where the women are so often plucky, expressive prodigies, and the men are ruminative, somewhat inarticulate geniuses. In this way, the film and its soundtrack might be similarly sorted. A great film is supposed to be somewhat diffuse, an accretion of subtle scenes culminating in a "Big Artistic Expression," a patriarchal mode of production. Meanwhile, a soundtrack is a film's emotional concentrate: all its pathos distilled in three-minute increments. If, as an object, a film is a brooding male lead, a soundtrack is a manic-pixie-dream girl, to use another trope from romantic films. The modern soundtrack holds both the score and the heartrending drama. In the space of the soundtrack, all time is delirium time.

The *Glitter* project has some interesting elements apart from its music. At one point, Dice says that he noticed Billie "ghosting" for Sylk (Padma Lakshmi), the star who lip-syncs her vocals. It's a surprising idea, ghost-singing for someone else, the demo artist as the musical first-draft writer, whose ego and credit die in the process of applying those things to others. Later in the film, Billie and Dice attend the "USA Music Awards," which must be a dupe for the American Music Awards; the idea of a fictional spectacle ghosting for another is intriguing, in the same way Toronto often stands in for New York City (parts of *Glitter* were shot in Toronto). There's also the big idea of the film, snuck into a throwaway scene: a stereotypical European music video director bellows, "The glitter can't overpower the artist," before walking over to Billie, who is posing uncomfortably in front of the camera, drowning in confetti. The *Glitter* period underlines that thought, as it applies to Carey's career, at least. In the years since, Carey has been serious about putting both herself and her art forward. In her autobiography, Carey writes that "songs are like monologues," and she's incorporated more filmmaking ideas in her music.

Like the *Glitter* soundtrack, Carey's 2009 song "It's a Wrap" resurfaced earlier this year, going viral on TikTok. "If I ever misrepresented my self-image, then I'm sorry," she croons, and you wonder if these lyrics about image-making are connected to her formative experience in movies. Later, she trills, "Boy, I'm checking the gate," making cinema jargon—the saying for assessing a camera for impurities or blockages—sound like a domestic duty, like taking out the trash or reviewing Ring footage. By the time she instructs her troubled lover to "watch the credits roll" in the final seconds, "It's a Wrap" has been recast as something far more fascinating than a mere breakup tune; instead, it's something like a DVD commentary in song, which explores the notion of a romantic relationship as a cinematic encounter. One of Carey's great skills as a songwriter is squeezing whole scenes into the tiniest of apertures, distilling the magnitude of experience into multisyllabic words like *acquiescent* and *elevator* and *denominator*. Carey, the comeback queen, consistently rescues herself from obscurity, making the celebrity acquaintance with exposure more legible. The *Glitter* debacle was the portent of the way women pop stars would be treated in the mainstream media, a specter of what was to come for Whitney Houston and Britney Spears. Do Carey's cinematic metaphors demonstrate a latent directorial drive? What if they merely underline the fact of an auteur all along? ✶

STUFF I'VE BEEN LISTENING TO

A QUARTERLY COLUMN, STEADY AS EVER

by Nick Hornby

ALBUMS MENTIONED:

✶ *Pretzel Logic*—Steely Dan
✶ *Woody's Winners*—Woody Herman
✶ *Center Stage*—Steve Gadd
✶ *Data Lords*—Maria Schneider
✶ *Our Natural World*—Maria Schneider

✶ *Allégresse*—Maria Schneider
✶ *Live at Sin-é*—Jeff Buckley
✶ *1969: Velvet Underground Live with Lou Reed*—Lou Reed
✶ *Fargo 1940*—Duke Ellington
✶ *Focus*—Stan Getz

It's June, and I'm in Birdland in New York City, for the third time in a week, waiting to see the Maria Schneider Orchestra, also for the third time in a week. It's not quite true to say that I see Maria Schneider whenever I get the chance—she's playing ten shows this week, five early, five late, so I'm missing seven of them— but when she's playing a residency, I go more than once. The shows are never the same, and the music is so complex anyway that you're never going to get to the bottom of it. Schneider is a composer and conductor whose music is somewhere between jazz and contemporary classical, and whose band consists of some of the best jazz musicians the United States has to offer. They don't play together regularly, and it's too expensive to ship them all to Europe (although I have seen her conduct European bands). These shows are big events in my cultural life.

Maybe there were little clues buried in my past that told me I would one day fall in love with big-band jazz. When I played Steely Dan's *Pretzel Logic*, I never once skipped the band's cover of "East St. Louis Toodle-Oo," even though it is a Duke Ellington song, albeit hardly a big-band rendition: Walter Becker imitated the trumpet through a voice box, and there was a pedal steel where a trombone should have been. And my love for Southside Johnny and the Asbury Jukes was never more intense than when the Jukes' horn section got close to what I would one day appreciate as Basie's punch.

But even so, I couldn't have anticipated that I'd one day bury myself in big-band music: Ellington and Count Basie, but also Woody Herman and Jimmy Heath, Marty Paich and Miles Davis's stuff with Gil Evans, Quincy Jones, and Gerald Wilson. It hasn't replaced Phoebe Bridgers or Jason Isbell or Lana Del Rey. I'm not one of those jazz fans who suddenly realizes that all rock and roll, or whatever you want to call it, is unsophisticated. In fact, "23 Red," say, from Herman's live album *Woody's Winners*, gives me the same kind of thrill that punk rock used to provide. There's a riff, and then the trumpeters let loose with a rapier-like set of controlled slashes. When the rest of the horns join in to egg them on with a sneaky, funky chart, they effectively set the Basin Street West jazz club, where the album was recorded, on fire. You can even hear a member of the audience let out a loud whistle, the kind that involves fingers, either because he's trying to express his excitement or because he's attempting to call the emergency service.

There's that kind of big-band music, and there's the Ellington kind, with its impossibly sophisticated charts and its rich, often melancholy colors, and

Illustration by Kristian Hammerstad

there's the funky kind—the drummer Steve Gadd made an album with the WDR Big Band that features covers of "Signed, Sealed, Delivered" and "I Can't Turn You Loose." There's something for everyone, and I can guarantee that if you like any kind of popular music, you'll find a big band for yourself.

I discovered Schneider because I was trying to find out who played with a large group here and now—as opposed to there and then, in the decades immediately before and after the Second World War—and the Grammy nominations were an unlikely and invaluable source of new big-band jazz. There are ninety-four Grammy categories, as you may or may not know, and one of them is the award for Best Large Jazz Ensemble Album. (The Steve Gadd album referred to above, *Center Stage*, was nominated in 2023.) Schneider has won seven Grammys in total—basically, she wins every time she puts out a record. One of her Grammys was for "Sue (or in a Season of Crime)," a collaboration with David Bowie—he was a fan too. The Maria Schneider Orchestra wasn't the big-band jazz I was looking for when I started poring over the Grammy small print, but it turned out to be the big-band jazz I needed: by turns modern, enthralling, complex, deeply moving.

There's a little bit you can listen to on Spotify, but Schneider is fighting a resolute battle against big tech. She wants us to pay for our music, so you can buy it properly only with proper money, as opposed to a subscription. Her last album, *Data Lords*, was a double album, with one set of dark, scary pieces about the power and control we have ceded to companies who have

only their own interests at heart; it feels like a soundtrack to the Upside Down in *Stranger Things*. The other CD is *Our Natural World*. It's benign and beautiful, and, in "Stone Song," incorporates a piece of sculptural art that was played at the Birdland shows. (At a previous residency, Schneider, a Central Park bird-watcher, provided several members of the audience with little wooden bird whistles.) I would never recommend my own work to you, but I would like to point you in the direction of a podcast I made with Schneider before the pandemic, for *BOMB* magazine. I was there only to get her to talk about her journey from Windom, Minnesota, a one-horse village, to writing charts for Gil Evans, and I managed that much, at least.

In Philip Glass's great memoir, *Words Without Music*, he describes how his father, who ran a small record store in Baltimore, would bring home contemporary classical records that never sold (the lack of sales cost him money) in order to understand why his customers hated them; young Philip sat on the stairs absorbing them in a different spirit, and a very particular career was born. Schneider was taught piano by a retired music teacher who had come to live in Windom. The woman,

who was equally at home with Rachmaninoff and stride piano, insisted on teaching little Maria music theory before she was allowed to begin lessons: another very particular career was born. Oh, there's one more element: her father was required to pilot small planes so he could fly to nearby flax fields. Music theory, the jazz-classical hybrid, that above-the-ground-among-the-birds perspective… We know we're the sum of our parts, but it's rare that you can see these parts given glorious expression.

The Birdland shows were, predictably, a joy, as they always are. You can choose where to focus your concentration, both visually and aurally, with a big band. You can spend a few minutes studying that horn section right there, just feet from your ears. (Maybe I should rephrase that: *just a couple of yards* from your ears. "Feet from your ears" sounds too weird. I'm trying to get you to imagine a concert, and all I give you is an unhelpful surrealist painting.) There's the apparently languid but superbly focused drummer, the accordionist, the guitar player, and Maria Schneider herself. There's no place for her on Birdland's tiny stage, and she frequently sits on the floor next to it, a beatific smile on

Ryuichi Sakamoto

her face, to listen to her soloists; when she's on her feet, she conducts compellingly with her hands and arms, apparently pulling and squeezing out tempo. The long pieces go all over the place, just as proper classical music does; this is as close as I'm going to get to classical music, I know now, but it'll do me. Perhaps I will convert, on my deathbed, just in case God really does prefer Bach and Beethoven to Drive-By Truckers and D'Angelo. (For how long do I have to listen to Bach to prove to Him that I'm serious? A couple of hours? The timing will be crucial.) But if He can't hear that the beautiful, thrilling "Hang Gliding," from Schneider's 2000 album *Allégresse*, is a tribute to Him and His works, then He needs to get over Himself.

Birdland holds a couple hundred people, so you can't be too far away from the stage, and the tickets were something like forty dollars, and Schneider is literally the best in the world at what she does; if you've recently paid a couple hundred bucks to watch some megastar on a screen at the, I don't know, the Sour Cream and Chive Pringles Arena, or the Walgreens Generic Zyrtec Stadium, I can only beg you to reexamine your cultural choices. The only downside to the great New York jazz clubs, and places like Ronnie Scott's in London, is that they are catnip to tourists: people think they have to go, at some point in their lives, and if they can attend only when Maria Schneider is performing, then so be it. This shouldn't bother me. They don't behave badly. They sit quietly and listen. But I would still prefer a system in which admittance is gained through written examination rather than first come, first served. Nothing rigorous—thirty short quiz questions followed by an essay—but enough to weed out the riffraff.

I have been thinking recently about how some of the most famous live recordings ever made were enjoyed by a very small number of people. The applause you can hear on Jeff Buckley's *Live at Sin-é*, the singer's first-ever release, was made by thirty or forty pairs of hands. The Village Vanguard—Bill Evans and Coltrane were among many artists whose shows there eventually became some of the greatest jazz albums of all time—has a capacity of one hundred and twenty-three. *1969: Velvet Underground Live with Lou Reed* was recorded at the Matrix in San Francisco (capacity one hundred) and at the End of Cole Ave., a club in Dallas (capacity unknown, but as the premises are now a restaurant, and nobody in Dallas would have known who the Velvets were back then, it's fair to assume there weren't thousands there, or even scores). My favorite big-band live recording is Ellington's *Fargo 1940*, the only one of the Duke's incredible Blanton-Webster band; two fans plonked a clunky recording device on the nightclub table in front of them, and forty years later won a Grammy for it.

Live music—live music in small, sweaty places—was what I missed most during the pandemic. I would have predicted that it would be live sports, but guess what? When hundreds of thousands of people are getting sick and dying, I needed no extra reason to be miserable. Music only ever makes me happy, unless I want it to make me angry or sad. I never want football to make me angry or sad, but it happens anyway. My team lets me down. When football did come back during lockdown, it was doubly dismal, because it was without the crowds, the very thing that gives it any meaning in the first place. Pro sports nearly died during the pandemic, at least in the UK; music, however, seemed to build up a head of steam. Artists made records, put little performances online, and created an apparently insatiable hunger for the live experience.

The feeling of a room lifting off as musicians lock in with one another and the audience is so precious that I can't believe concerts used to happen without me before COVID. I am trying to make sure that doesn't happen again. That week in New York City I saw the three shows at Birdland, a Ben Folds show at the Beacon, and a surprise full-band Santana show after a screening of the new (and very good) documentary at the Tribeca Festival. At the Juan-les-Pins jazz festival in France, I saw a young musical genius, North London's own Jacob Collier; a wonderful, uproarious French funk band called Deluxe; and the ubiquitous Chic, Angélique Kidjo, Branford Marsalis, and Brad Mehldau. Just last week I saw HAIM play to a deliriously devoted crowd in London. And last night, I didn't go to see the Unthanks, the English folk band whose relationship to traditional music is not dissimilar to Maria Schneider's to jazz. I didn't go, because I had COVID, which kind of brings us full circle. I'll be back in action later in the week, if I test negative. Nubya Garcia is performing Stan Getz's *Focus* album in London. I'm never not going again. ✴

CLOSE READ

UNPACKING ONE REDOUBTABLE PASSAGE. IN THIS ISSUE: THE FIRST TWO VERSES OF
THE 1927 RECORDING "BLESSED ARE THE POOR IN SPIRIT" BY LUTHER MAGBY

by Mike McGonigal

The song has the purest of sentiments. Its chorus repeats five times. That first line is from the Beatitudes: "Blessed are the poor in spirit, for theirs is the kingdom of heaven." Yes, this is where that "The meek shall inherit the earth" bit comes from. I believe the phrase "children of the heavenly king" appeared first as the opening to a hymn by John Cennick in his 1742 collection Sacred Hymns for the Children of God, in the Days of Their Pilgrimage. And the phrase "crown in glory" likely comes from the "crown of glory" one finds in Peter 5:4.

Luther Magby recorded two songs in Atlanta on November 11, 1927. They were issued as a ten-inch, 78 rpm disc by Columbia Records just a few months later. Very few original copies of this record still exist.

The best-known of all the early guitar evangelists and street corner musicians was the genius Blind Willie Johnson, who sang in either a deep bass or his natural alto, while his slide guitar skills would have brought in any listener from blocks away. The only known photograph of Johnson shows a tin cup firmly affixed to the headstock of his instrument. His instrumental rendition of an a capella lining hymn, "Dark Was the Night, Cold Was the Ground," is included on the Voyager's Golden Record, currently floating well beyond our solar system.

The gruff vocalist seems to have stuffed his mumbly mouth with cotton balls, while the up-tempo harmonium sounds like the organ from some carnival ride. It's worked at with feverish percussion, alongside the one-man-band flourish of a tambourine accompaniment. A brief coda toward the end sounds like circus tap dancing music—it's sublime.

Blessed are the poor in spirit,
children of the heavenly king.
We shall wear a crown in glory,
Lord, when on Earth our work is done.

If you can't sing like angels,
yeah, or you can't pray like Paul,
you will know the love of Jesus
'Cause that I say, he died for us all.

If you were a street performer—both as a way to make a living and because you were compelled to spread "the good news"—how might you raise yourself above the constant ruckus of a 1920s urban center? You would play louder and gruffer, or you would just sound absolutely out of this universe in order to cut through competing cries from the ragpickers, the cobblers, and the vegetable sellers.

In 1927, modern gospel music had not yet coalesced, but hundreds of artists were inspired to attach sanctified messages to jazzy, bluesy, and jug-band-infused sounds. Many were inspired by the nascent Pentecostal revival movement, which held that anyone could go forth and preach, regardless of race or sex. This music is often retroactively referred to as "sanctified blues." It was cutting-edge stuff; note the vernacular lyrics to "Blessed": it has the poetry of the King James Version, but was written in street patois too.

Did I get this part right? It took multiple relistenings to transcribe it properly; finally, my transcription was reinforced by a forum on weeniecampbell.com. In the internet age, mistakes tend to linger. Writing about Magby in All Music Guide two decades ago, musician Eugene Chadbourne made the claim that "in 2002, he was still maintaining a busy performing schedule." Clearly, Chadbourne was mistaken. (It was likely the son, Luther C., performing.) As All Music Guide provides metadata and short reviews for many online sources, this misinformation lives on.

OCCUPATION:
Farmer, General Farm

We have no photos of the artist, and know only a few facts from US Census reports (thankfully, Magby is an obscure enough name). He was born in South Carolina in 1896 and died in Dalhart, Texas, in 1966. At the time of the 1920 census, he and his wife, Mamie, plus a one-year-old son, Luther C., still resided in South Carolina. Luther's occupation was recorded as "Farmer, General Farm." The allure of artists who make just one great record cannot be overstated.

Blind Mamie and A. C. Forehand sang in the higher registers and employed a strategically played service bell in their songs. Reverend Edward Clayborn's staccato rhythms and stunted vocals belie gorgeous fingerpicking and call-and-response-style slide guitar. Washington Phillips's high-pitched morality plays dance above a zither-like dolceola, sounding like some celestial ice cream truck. ✶

13

ASK CARRIE

A QUARTERLY COLUMN FROM
CARRIE BROWNSTEIN, WHO IS BETTER
AT DISPENSING ADVICE THAN TAKING IT

Send questions to advice@thebeliever.net

Q: *Whenever I fall in love with a new song, or an old song that's new to me, I can't stop playing it on repeat. It's the only thing I listen to while on runs, in my car, or walking to class. Even in the presence of others, I play the song over and over again. Eventually, after several days or even weeks, this honeymoon phase abruptly ends, and the song starts to annoy me. I can't help wondering if this burn-through-it approach is problematic. Would it be better if I didn't listen on repeat, perhaps allowing for a more sustained relationship with the songs I fall for? Or are my indulgences exactly why these songs are made?* —Gabe Boyd, Oceanside, CA

A: I don't think it's better to manufacture a more sustained relationship with the songs you love. The beauty of music is that we can let it destroy us without needing years of therapy. So go ahead and let these songs love-bomb you, tease and seduce you, inspire someone to yell *Get a room!*, tear your heart out and leave you for dead. Or, you know, just hold your hand and take you on a leisurely walk. When the song gets on your nerves, move on! Without tears, without processing! If I were you, I'd continue to live fully in the moment with the music you love. After all, if they're great songs, destined for timelessness, you'll find them again. Best of all, when you get back together, there will be little judgment or confusion from your friends.

Q: *Please help me curate a playlist. My dinner parties are terrible. Please.*
Dev
Richmond, VA

A: Here you go. (I'm much better at playlists than cooking, BTW, so thanks for splitting the hosting duties with me.)

- Arthur Russell: "Make 1, 2"
- Caribou: "Bees"
- Pasteur Lappe: "Sanaga Calypso"
- Joe Jackson: "You Can't Get What You Want (Till You Know What You Want)"
- Alex G: "Runner"
- The Monochrome Set: "He's Frank (Slight Return)"
- Wire: "The 15th"
- Cochemea: "Mimbreños"
- The Gun Club: "Mother of Earth"
- Talk Talk: "Give It Up"
- Carol Cool: "Upside Down"
- Dee Sharp: "Rising to the Top"
- Neu!: "Isi"
- Rosanne Cash: "Seven Year Ache"
- Bryan Ferry: "Let's Stick Together"
- Rufus: "Circles"
- Orville Peck: "Dead of Night"
- Yola: "Shady Grove"
- Fleetwood Mac: "Big Love"
- Robert Wyatt: "At Last I Am Free"

Illustration by Kristian Hammerstad

Q: *I've always taken pride in my diverse musical taste. I enjoy building my repertoire, seeking out new artists and genres from radically different traditions. But recently this has changed. The only thing I seem to be able to listen to is soft rock from the 1970s. Give me Jackson Browne's sweet, world-weary melancholia. Give me "Ventura Highway" and the wind in my hair, or Steely Dan to light my way. This music wraps me in a warm blanket that inoculates me against the world. But it's becoming a problem. I'm cocooning myself in nostalgia for an era I wasn't even alive for, at the expense of fostering attachments to contemporary artists who can speak to the present moment. How can I rekindle my passion for the unfamiliar, alien, and cutting-edge in music?*

"Helplessly Hoping" for your advice,
Caleb
Brooklyn, NY

A: Your fear of the nostalgia trap is a common one. When we have David Bowie, Prince, Otis Redding, Joni Mitchell, the Clash, Nirvana, Nina Simone, and Bruce Springsteen (the list could go on and on; I actually had a hard time stopping), why do we need, well, anything else? Even when an artist isn't canonical, a one-hit wonder to which you danced in middle school (cue "Waiting for a Star to Fall" by Boy Meets Girl) can land in a way no contemporary pop song ever will. I relate to the desire to wrap oneself in the familiar, to know what's coming next, to eschew the discomfort of the unfamiliar. The present day takes effort, a witnessing and a wrestling. As for the future, dread often outweighs optimism. Whether we were around for it or not, there is comfort in what is done, codified, and settled upon. Solution-wise, I hesitate to recommend an algorithm for discovering new music, a.k.a. streaming-service playlists, which lend themselves to conformity and often overlook deeper cuts, and by "deeper" I literally mean an album's second or third track. Instead, might I suggest you ask a handful of friends or colleagues to give you a list of five contemporary musicians and/or songs they love? Then, if you can, spend some time with these artists. Listen in the background, on the subway, in the car, and see what stands out. Seek out entire albums by the bands to which you're drawn and give those a listen. As for myself, I try to make a handful of playlists every year that include contemporary artists. At the end of the year, even if it's only a song or two, I end up loving some of these songs enough to merge them with my perennial favorites. Ultimately, though, I wouldn't worry too much about your musical taste; many older songs actually *do* speak to the present moment, just as many current songs do not. We love music that finds us where we're at, so maybe just broaden who and what can find you.

NONEXHAUSTIVE LIST OF MUSIC THAT HAS BEEN PLAYED IN OUTER SPACE

✳ "Watching the Sky and Thinking a Thought" by Mykhailo Petrenko and Vladislav Zaremba
✳ "Jingle Bells" by James Lord Pierpont
✳ "Heartbreak Hotel" by Elvis Presley
✳ "Space Oddity" and "Life on Mars?" by David Bowie
✳ "Dōngfāng hóng" (The East Is Red) by Li Youyuan
✳ "The Fountain in the Park" by Ed Haley
✳ *Space Opera* by Didier Marouani
✳ *Delicate Sound of Thunder* by Pink Floyd
✳ "Beagle 2" by Blur
✳ "Reach for the Stars" by will.i.am
✳ *1989* by Taylor Swift
✳ "Higher Power" by Coldplay
✳ "Dynamite" by BTS
✳ "SORATO" by Sakanaction
✳ "Johnny B. Goode" by Chuck Berry
✳ "Across the Universe" by the Beatles
✳ "Lalala," "Bald James Deans," "Hot Times," and "No Love" by Julien Civange and Louis Haéri
✳ "Mythodea" by Vangelis
✳ Symphony no. 5, first movement, by Ludwig van Beethoven
✳ "Up in the Air" by Thirty Seconds to Mars

—list compiled by Emily Lang

Q: *My friend recently suggested that I have a tendency to form intimate attachments to musical artists based on their being underappreciated. After she said it, I agreed that I hear music differently when it is obscure. There's a special quality to it. I enjoy feeling like a steward of these musicians and their art, tasked with keeping their dim candle alight while everyone's attention is elsewhere. The problem comes when they gain any kind of clout—my experience of their music dulls and I give them up. Why can't I just enjoy this music I love with the rest of the world? How do I live with or without the churlish influence of my inner hipster?*

Best,
Charlie
Indianapolis, IN

A: I appreciate how old-school this conundrum is. Part of me wants you to really own it and just start brandishing the term *sellout* to any band with more than ten thousand monthly listeners on Spotify, who're playing anything bigger than three-hundred-person-capacity clubs, or who've had the audacity to build a website. Forming intimate emotional attachments to musical artists is part of being a fan, and I'm sure most songwriters aim to foment a deep and personal connection between their music and the listener. However—and this goes for anything and anyone you love—no one's candle should remain dim! I can't imagine any of the artists you love making their vision board or talking to their friends/bandmates/partners about their career and saying things like: *My dream is to have Charlie in Indianapolis like my songs plus maybe twenty other people. Total. Forever.* Or: *Obscurity is our brand.* Or: *The best way to write music is after coming home from my other three jobs.* My advice: celebrate the fact that you're a seeker and an early adopter and let the rest go. But if you want to keep that inner hipster alive, you can definitely cling to the following sentiment: *I only like their first two albums.*

Q: *My boyfriend "gave me" one of his beats for my birthday. I'm trying hard not to be petty about it, but I feel somewhat disrespected, considering that for his birthday I bought him these expensive headphones I knew he really wanted. It just feels like I was an afterthought to his studio time, though he seems to genuinely consider it a meaningful gift. After he watched me listen, he got clued in to the fact that I was upset, and became gloomy. I ended up having to reassure him that I think his music is great and was happy with his effort. Are you convinced this is the thoughtful present he says it is? Am I just being ungrateful?*

Yours,
Martine
Burlington, VT

A: The fact that you are asking this question makes me think you already know the answer, or know the answer you want. Also, you put "gave me" in quotes, which implies you feel like you weren't actually given anything. I can see how receiving "birthday beats" could felt a bit tossed off and random. Like a chef bringing home the kitchen leftovers and acting like the food had been cooked for you. Thoughtful, yes, but a gift? Perhaps the difference between a gesture and a present has to do with intention and context. Particularly on birthdays, and definitely if it matters to you! While it sounds sweet to have your partner share his music with you, my guess is you feel like the beats weren't created with you in mind and therefore don't measure up to your expectations. This really boils down to communication. If your boyfriend doesn't know what you like, gift-wise—within reason, of course; not all of us can afford things like a trip to Italy, or to space—then let him know. That way you won't be disappointed, and he won't be insulted when you don't jump for joy over a 180 BPM, woodblock-heavy groove that was originally intended for a Post Malone collab. ✴

Peter Tosh

UNDERWAY

WE ASK WRITERS AND ARTISTS: WHAT'S ON YOUR DESK? WHAT ARE YOU WORKING ON?

by Thao Nguyen

Resistance band

To counteract guitar, piano, and inward folding. On breaks I go outside and stretch and strengthen my scapulae. Also, ankle stability!

One of my Yamaha studio monitors

Great for listening back, mixing, a reprieve from clingy headphones. Ordered the wrong size by mistake but that was six years ago.

Photo

My mom in her late twenties, when she worked for the South Vietnamese embassy. Helps keep the dream alive.

Universal Audio Apollo Twin

My go-to interface. I record vocals, guitar, synthesizers, drum machines through it. True workhorse, travels well. Is this Tape Op (recording engineer magazine)?!

Beyerdynamic headphones

For recording. I treasure them for their luxurious cushioning and snug fit, but sometimes it's true that there can be too much of a good thing.

Prayer beads

These were my grandmother's. She helped raise me. I meditate and pray and sometimes worry with them.

Buddha statue

Travels with me. I set it out in every hotel room, etc. At home it's on my desk for comfort and calm.

I am writing songs for my next album. The last one, *Temple*, was released in May of 2020. I'm in the midst of finding out what this collection of songs will be: their cadences, their heat. I zero in on sonic nature and emotional content by imagining how I'll want to be in communication with the audience, in both recorded and live settings, and how I want to be moving, what kind of escape and grounding I'm looking for onstage. For me, the early generative phase must be rife with in-house vigilance. It is too easy to start a song and never finish it. Before, I'd find too much comfort and exhilaration in having new ideas and never really pursuing them. It was fear, making it hard to truly be in service of any one thing. People cannot trust people who traffic only in ideas; you'll get a reputation. ✶

Illustration by Kristian Hammerstad

A BRIEF AND ANNOYING HISTORY OF KAZOO ORCHESTRAS

(HEY, WHERE ARE YOU GOING?? COME BACK!)

by Paul Collins

A membranophone belonging to the mirliton (or "eunuch flute") family, the kazoo has a deep and profound history; and of the playing of many kazoos at once, we find a correlative history even deeper and more profound. In 1667, John Milton wrote of a massed kazoo chorus:

> At length a universal hubbub wilde
> Of stunning sounds and voices all confus'd
> Born through the hollow dark assaults his eare
> With loudest vehemence…
> And Tumult and Confusion all imbroil'd,
> And Discord with a thousand various mouths.

Some will argue, correctly, that Milton is in fact describing hell and its torments. But that's only because the kazoo hadn't been invented yet.

1882: Mysterious newspaper ads tout the Elkazoo, a miraculous new instrument: "The great Egyptian musical wonder. Original discovered among the ruins of the pyramids.… Astonishing it may seem, those can play on the Elkazoo that play on no other instrument." Its New Hampshire manufacturer may be connected to prior ads hawking a "Vienna Eolian Labial Organ."

1883: Warren Herbert Frost receives US Patent 270,543 for a "Toy or Musical Instrument." He claims that "this instrument, to which I propose to give the name 'kazoo,'" can "produce imitations of birds and animals, as the caw of a crow, the crow of the cock, the moo of a cow, &c." Wisely, he makes no further mention of music in the filing.

1884: Public events across the country are overrun by kazoo bands: a steamboat excursion in Boston, an electrical exhibition in Philadelphia, but above all, political rallies. Kazoo bands appear at election-night celebrations for Grover Cleveland in Indiana, Vermont, and South Carolina. "The inventor would be hanged, drawn, quartered and burnt," reports a Washington, DC, newspaper, "but it is more than likely that he is kept out of the way in some insane asylum."

1886: A Lafayette College student editorializes against the "barbarous dissonance" of a new campus ensemble: "The Kazoo band seems bent on doing their serenading when others want to study."

1887: Kazoos are exported to London, where ads run for "The New Intense American Musical Instrument."

1888: Election-year kazoo bands return like locusts. From the Democratic State Convention in Indiana comes a report of a forty-piece group "practicing regularly during the past two weeks, except as it has been interfered with by the police."

1889: Kazoos are sold in India by Charles Gould & Co., which suggests buying four at a time, as "choruses using the Kazoo invariably receive repeated encores."

1894: The popular American stage production *Blue Jeans* promises audiences both a "Kazoo Orchestra" and an "Intensely Thrilling Sawmill Scene," though regrettably not at the same time.

1894: While a freshman at Yale, composer Charles Ives pens "A Son of the Gambolier," which includes a "Kazoo Chorus." He graduates with a D+ average.

1895: Warren Herbert Frost files to patent the Zobo, which is regarded as a somewhat improved kazoo, or perhaps simply a less unimproved one.

1896: Zobo bands form nationwide, including organized regiments of bicyclists, worryingly combining two current crazes. A young H. P. Lovecraft joins one band, later recalling: "I was a member of the Blackstone Military band… a star zobo soloist." Its effect on Lovecraft's development is not recorded.

1900: In an act of Brutus-like treachery, the Zobo Company secretary-treasurer, Louis Crakow, defects to create a Zobo knockoff: the Sonophone, or Song-O-Phone.

1901: Zobo ads target poor churches, assuring them that with enough Zobos, "A GRAND PIPE ORGAN EFFECT CAN BE OBTAINED" for "those with no pipe organ." Similar ads for the Sonophone claim, not very convincingly, that this effect can be achieved with a quartet.

1902: George D. Smith patents a submarine-shaped metal kazoo, ushering in the modern instrument.

1907: A metal workshop that will become the Original Kazoo Company is founded in the Buffalo suburb of Eden, New York, producing kazoos based on the Smith model. For the next three decades, the kazoo, the Zobo, and the Sonophone battle for atonal supremacy.

1914: As wartime shipping lanes become uncertain, the Sonophone Company trumpets a new message to retailers: "THE SONOPHONE FILLS THE PLACE OF OTHER TOYS."

1919: An ad in *The Singapore Free Press* reads: "With a Song-O-Phone you can throw a crowd into convulsions of laughter, astonish everybody, no matter how wise they are, frighten away burglars, secure sound sleep in spite of the snorer in the next room, win a victory in battle, win a girl's heart, win a husband, square yourself coming home late, make a family happy, keep the young folks at home, pleasantly pass the long winter evenings on the farm, quickly put a child to sleep, be 'IT' at the sea-side or on the Mountains, cure everybody of the blues, and make everybody remember you with gratitude for life."

1920: "Juvenile jazz bands"—marching bands of children dressed in military-style uniforms, playing in tight formation on kazoos and drums—form in mining towns in England and Wales. Like colliery brass bands, these are organized largely by miners.

1924: A "Kazoo Symphony" performs on KDKA radio in Pittsburgh, making kazoos inescapable even in the safety of one's living room.

1928: The *Ziegfeld Follies* employs more than eighty Song-O-Phones in a stage production. In what is surely only a coincidence, one year later the world economy collapses.

1930: The US government, considering whether imported kazoos should be subject to a 40 percent tariff on instruments or a 70 percent tariff on toys, makes it official: "A kazoo is not a musical instrument."

1930s: The Batistes, the famed musical family of New Orleans, form the Dirty Dozen Kazoo Band, initially to parade "all over town whenever boxer Joe Louis won a bout." The kazoo becomes a fixture of Mardi Gras for the next fifty years.

1943: The Original Kazoo Company halts production for two years so that its sheet metal can be put to less destructive uses.

1949: Art Mooney and His Orchestra release "Doo De Doo on an Old Kazoo," an experiment in kazoo maximalism. It is their first hit single to fail to reach the Top 20.

1951: The London trade paper *Melody Maker* claims the kazoo was invented by "Alabama Vest, an American Negro, circa 1840" and "built to his specifications by Thaddeus von Clegg, a German clockwinder of many attainments." No source is given, and neither name appears in the records. In addition to their suspiciously Roald Dahl–like names, one might consider the name in the article's byline: "Parp Green."

1963: Thomas Pynchon's novel *V.* features "an unemployed musicologist named Petard who had dedicated his life to finding the lost Vivaldi Kazoo Concerto." *The Crying of Lot 49* (1966) begins with the opus.

1971: The Pelaw Hussars appear in the British film *Get Carter*, in which uniformed children march with kazoos before a naked and shotgun-wielding Michael Caine. This remains the definitive cinematic appearance of a juvenile jazz band.

1972: Pierre Boulez refuses to conduct David Bedford's new composition "With 100 Kazoos," as it entails handing out kazoos to the audience. "He rejected my piece on the grounds that audiences would be stupid and would fool about with their kazoos in the other pieces too," Bedford later explains.

1973: The band Kazoophony is formed by six musicians from the Eastman School of Music in Rochester, New York. They perform such compositions as "The William to Hell Overture" at Avery Fisher Hall and Carnegie Hall in New York City, and at the truck terminal opening at the Emerson Street Dump in Rochester.

1978: The fledgling Rhino Records releases *Some Kazoos* by the Temple City Kazoo Orchestra. Purportedly recorded at the Temple City Moose Hall in California, the EP includes a cover of "Whole Lotta Love" that utterly destroys Led Zeppelin's swaggering epic. It begins with just one kazoo, then two, then three, then four, and then *Oh my god the vocal part*. It is an atrocity and an act of genius; it is both the *Hindenburg* and the *Mona Lisa* of kazoo recordings.

1979: The Temple City Kazoo Orchestra performs on *The Mike Douglas Show* in an episode costarring David Brenner, Cheryl Tiegs, and Lou Ferrigno. They later play on Dinah Shore's show, which they complain has lousy catering.

c. 1981: The Original Kazoo Company switches from buzzing animal-gut membranes to pink mylar. Defending the change, the company's president notes that they previously also switched away from lead paint.

1983: Kazoophony cofounder Barbara Stewart publishes *How to Kazoo*, which sells more than one hundred thousand copies. Her book repeats the *Melody Maker* tale of Alabama Vest and Thaddeus von Clegg. References to both begin to creep into newspapers, books, and articles, and eventually into the Wikipedia entry for "kazoo."

1985: A crowd of thirty-five thousand at the Virginia Tech–Vanderbilt halftime show provides kazoo accompaniment to the Oak Ridge Boys on their hit "Elvira."

2000: Composer John Powell uses a kazoo orchestra on the soundtrack to *Chicken Run* and presents the result to DreamWorks executive Jeffrey Katzenberg. "The first time we tried it," Powell noted in an interview, "he turned to me and said, 'What the fuck are you doing?' And then two weeks later he was asking us to put more kazoos in."

2007: The Original Kazoo Company celebrates one hundred years of greater Buffalo–Niagara Falls metropolitan area dominance in kazoo production.

2013: Rhino Records cofounder Harold Bronson reveals in his memoir that the Temple City Kazoo Orchestra included himself, fellow Rhino founder Richard Foos, and "members of Stevie Wonder's band."

2019: Fans of local metal band Lamb of God descend with kazoos on Richmond, Virginia, to drown out a Westboro Baptist Church protest against a transgender legislator.

2023: A water-damaged and autographed Temple City Kazoo Orchestra EP turns up on eBay. It bears this inscription: "Andrew, invest in therapy." ✶

SONGS THAT SAMPLE TOM TOM CLUB'S "GENIUS OF LOVE"

✶ "Big Energy" by Latto
✶ "Return of the Mack" by Mark Morrison
✶ "Fantasy" by Mariah Carey
✶ "No Pause" by Girl Talk
✶ "It's Nasty" by Grandmaster Flash and the Furious Five
✶ "Genius Rap" by Dr. Jekyll and Mr. Hyde
✶ "Brick City Mashin'!" by Redman
✶ "So International" by B-Legit feat. Too $hort
✶ "That's the Way" by DJ Clue feat. Mase, Fabolous, and Foxy Brown

—list compiled by Bryce Woodcock

A SHORT INTERVIEW WITH NATALIE MERCHANT

LOOKING BACK AT *IN MY TRIBE*, NEARLY FOUR DECADES AFTER ITS RELEASE

"*A*ll is memory taken home with me," sings Natalie Merchant at the close of 10,000 Maniacs' 1987 album, In My Tribe. *The song, "Verdi Cries," captures a young person's experience of listening to an opera recording through the walls of a hotel, eavesdropping on lives rich with culture and years, aching to share their passions. That plaintive yearning for worldly wisdom juxtaposed with poignant self-awareness—a contradictory mark of young adulthood—shines through every song on this record. Of all the music that best captures that golden moment of my own life, it's this complete album, song by song, that I go back to the most, without skipping.*

Listening to In My Tribe *on a beautiful summer drive in 2022, I realized the album had been released thirty-five years ago. Merchant herself was only twenty-two when it was recorded. Given the long and rich career that she has enjoyed as a solo artist and activist in the decades since, and her time as the lead singer and songwriter for 10,000 Maniacs, I wondered how she remembered this seminal album. To me, it's vivid with songs that build on one another like an eclectic analog archive of Technicolor postcards, bittersweet snapshots, or handwritten letters home, each note sparking memories. Did she feel the same? I reached out to request to speak with Natalie Merchant about the album, and much to my delight, she accepted. During our conversation, Merchant traced her sentimental education and offered a glimpse into the motivations of an artist who continues to not only create vital art (like her new album,* Keep Your Courage, *released in spring 2023) but also tour and perform in support of causes as much as for her music.*
—Lauren LeBlanc

THE BELIEVER: You grew up in the small city of Jamestown, New York: it had to be a shock to tour nationwide as a musician. What was that like?

NATALIE MERCHANT: I'd been to Buffalo once. [*Laughs*] I went to Manhattan on a school trip once. I'd been nowhere.

I believe the second time I was ever in an airplane, I was flying to England to make *The Wishing Chair* [Merchant's first album for Elektra Records, released in 1985]. The first time was on a brief tour in England before recording that album. The band really opened up the world for me. And I traveled and met so many interesting people. And found a way to express myself.

BLVR: You were a community college student when you joined the band 10,000 Maniacs. For financial reasons, you opted to postpone an undergraduate education in New York City in order to avoid debt. Could you talk about that?

NM: Get on the tour bus, or go to college and go into debt. I thought, Well, I'll just get on the tour bus and travel. It was kind of my equivalent of a gap year, because by the time I was eighteen, I had an associate's degree because of Advanced Placement classes. So I thought, Well, you know, I did two years of college already, I'm only eighteen. Let's see what traveling is like and meeting people and playing music. And then I never went back to college.

BLVR: At age twenty-two, when you should have been a fresh college graduate, you wrote and composed *In My Tribe*. How did it feel to be aware of that?

NM: I was talking to my daughter recently about how I've been on every major college campus in this country, but I was working. I was the same age as the people at the colleges. And at the time, I don't know if I really recognized that, because I felt like college just wasn't an option for me because I had chosen my career and I was doing it. But I felt intimidated. We'd play at Harvard or Stanford or Berkeley or UCLA. We played all the colleges because we were college-radio darlings, but I didn't feel like college could ever be possible for me.

BLVR: But you never stopped learning and being inquisitive. How did you stay engaged on the road?

Illustration by Kristian Hammerstad

NM: I was a voracious reader. I was self-educating. So I'd be reading Tolstoy and Dostoyevsky, and I read all the Henry Miller novels and Anaïs Nin, and I remember reading all those Jack Kerouac books when I was eighteen or nineteen years old: *The Subterraneans*, *The Dharma Bums*, *On the Road*. I remember I liked Jane and Paul Bowles a lot, Flannery O'Connor, Kafka, *Madame Bovary*, *Lady Chatterley's Lover*, the Alexandria Quartet. I was reading history, a lot of current-events books to educate myself in every way I could. I had a subscription to *The Nation* and *The Progressive*. I was such a dedicated reader when I was younger, I was like a sponge. I was always reading in the back of the bus, in the dressing room or cafés, wherever. All my friends had gone to college or were going to college; they would just tell me what to read.

BLVR: *In My Tribe* is such a beautiful album about recognizing your place in the world and learning to use your voice to speak out. What was it like writing that album?

NM: I wrote that record when I was twenty years old, and my daughter is in her twenties now. Her level of sophistication is much greater than mine was at that age. I think kids today are a lot more sophisticated because there's a lot more information that's available to them. At that time, the world was opening up to me. I wrote songs about Jack Kerouac and the Painted Desert—I had just been to the West for the first time—because I was writing about what I knew. "Cherry Tree" was a song about my grandfather's illiteracy. He had been an immigrant and his father was an invalid. And at the age of eight or nine, my grandfather went to work in the coal mines in Pennsylvania. Because his father was bedridden, he and his siblings had to go to work, so he never learned to read or write—yet he was a very proud man. "City of Angels" was about being in Los Angeles. Coming from a very small town in the Northeast, I was always shocked by going to Los Angeles. It was like going to Babylon. My guitar player—I remember we went for a hike one day in LA and he got up above the Hollywood Hills, and as he looked down he said, "Front-row seat to the apocalypse." And then he said, "This looks like a good place for a crucifix." "Don't Talk" was about alcoholism, "Gun Shy" was about my brother. My poor brother! I actually named him, and

he was still in the military, obviously. He got so much flak for that song. He was stationed in Germany. People would hear the song and they would torture him over it: "So good at making soldiers, but they're not as good at making men." I was really disappointed with him for joining the military. "My Sister Rose" is about my aunt Rose and her husband, Rocky. It's about growing up in a second-generation Italian American family and those weddings that I remember from my childhood in the '60s and '70s, which were huge affairs and big family events, where you got to see your grandmother and her sisters, you know, drinking and dancing. It was really uncharacteristic! There was "A Campfire Song," which was about waking up to power dynamics in the world, and resources.

BLVR: What is it like to listen to the album now?

NM: Anytime I hear anything recorded before *Tigerlily*, I just say, "Oh, little Natalie" [*laughs*] because I sound like a little cartoon animal. I just sound so young and high-pitched and tentative in my delivery. They're like embarrassing journals. My voice has gotten deeper and richer and I'm less hurried in my delivery. But I was just learning how to write songs and make records at the time, and the production on those early records, especially *In My Tribe*, is a little brittle for my ear, because it was the early days for digital recording. And these are the things that really are killjoys when you talk to a musician about their work, because you probably never paid attention to the production. But the first thing I hear is this kind of sizzly early digital production. To its credit, I thought it was a very ambitious record, lyrically, and I'm proud of a lot of the phrases on the record and the variety of subject matter, and it did stand out. Time has really changed the way people look at me. At the time, I was an oddball, because I was writing socially conscious lyrics and I was a vegetarian. I did as many benefit concerts as I did paying concerts, and it was just—I had a lot of concerns. And it was a time when I think everyone just expected something more frivolous from musicians. Now, you know, all that is pretty much accepted as a given: you're supposed to have concerns and you're supposed to be a vegan.

Photo by Jacob Blickenstaff.

BLVR: What was it like to be a young working musician traveling to Los Angeles to record this album? Did you have an apartment there? Where did the studio put you up?

NM: So the label put us up in a place called Oakwood Apartments. There's several of them around LA and they have cottage cheese ceilings. Single room, wall-to-wall carpet, mildewy. Yeah, everything was concrete and mildew and wall-to-wall carpeting. And I felt very alienated by the whole environment. And I remember walking to the studio one day and when I got there, they had to give me oxygen. They told me no one walks in LA. I remember Peter Asher [legendary record producer who worked with the Beatles, James Taylor, and Linda Ronstadt, among other artists] had a couple of young children. And his wife and his kids lived out in Malibu, and I remember they had a guest house. And he felt sorry for me, I think, after that incident, and started taking me home with him at night.

And I would sleep in the guest house and I could get up in the morning and walk on the beach. And then we would come back to the studio together. My only experience of a Malibu beach house up till that point had been my friend's Barbie's house.

So it was pretty crazy. And I remember the fee that Asher received was three times my mother's annual salary. And I remember calling Jefferson Holt, who managed R.E.M., and I was in tears. I was like, "I don't understand anything." And he said, "Believe me, Peter Asher is going to earn that money." And he said, "And your mother makes minimum wage." You know, my mother was a secretary. I didn't understand—the scale of things was unclear to me. Now it makes perfect sense. I've paid producers the same or more since, but it was shocking at that moment.

BLVR: Who were you hanging out with? And what was that kind of time like socially? Were you just writing a

Photo by Jacob Blickenstaff.

a big collector of folk art. So he and Stipe introduced me to folk art. The first time I ever went to New Orleans was with R.E.M. on tour for *In My Tribe*, and Michael [Stipe] took me to a folk art gallery and the dealer had just acquired a stack of about fifty Henry Darger paintings. And Michael [Stipe] wouldn't buy any, because he thought they were creepy and had bad juju. I remember he and I stayed up all night after the show, wandering around. And we got a temporary fish tattoo and cut it in half. He got the tail and I got the head. I just remember it was so hot, one of those hot New Orleans nights where there's no way to sleep after the show. We were just so full of adrenaline. I have such vivid memories of that.

BLVR: What were you listening to at the time that you recorded *In My Tribe*?

NM: It was probably a lot of Anglo and Celtic folk music. I had just spent a year living in London. Sandy Denny and Fairport Convention, Richard and Linda Thompson, Dolores Keane, June Tabor, Maddy Prior, the Bothy Band, Shirley Collins and the Albion Band, Steeleye Span, Anne Briggs. I loved the Strawbs and Nick Drake. As far as contemporaries: Talking Heads, the Smiths, Billy Bragg, the Cure, Cocteau Twins, Peter Gabriel, Sinéad O'Connor, Tom Waits. I think that was around the time I discovered Nina Simone and Harry Smith's *Anthology of American Folk Music*.

BLVR: Did you feel encouraged or pushed to consider other directions regarding your music and songwriting?

NM: I don't remember anyone trying to push me anywhere. I was upset when the label put out "Peace Train" as the first single. "Peace Train" was a song that Peter Asher came to see us play in Buffalo when he was considering whether to produce us or not, and it was New Year's Eve, I think. And we played "Peace Train" as a New Year's song. Something optimistic. And he just latched on to it. Like, *That's your first single!* And we all said, "But we wrote all these other songs!"

I always felt like I was more cynical than "Peace Train." The message of "Peace Train," although sweet, was naive and unrealistic and, I felt, not that nuanced. I really felt like the songs I was writing were more grounded in reality and just meant more to me. So I was disappointed. We made a stupid video for it. It got buried. ★

ton of letters and reading and taking in the view in Los Angeles? Or how much of the city did you see if you were spending most of your time in the studio?

NM: The main question is: What do you do in Los Angeles if you don't have a car? [*Laughs*] We were working pretty steadily. And I remember R.E.M. was there for some of that time because I remember hanging out. Michael [Stipe] came to the studio to sing on "A Campfire Song." We had a mutual friend, Michael Meister, who owns Texas Records in Santa Monica. And we had met Michael—both of us had met him—because Texas was this cool independent record store, and he would have shows there. And he was tied in with KCRW. I would go to Santa Monica and Michael [Stipe] would come pick me up. And then I'd go hang out with him. [Michael Meister] was

DOMINO RECORDING COMPANY 2023

CAT POWER
CAT POWER SINGS DYLAN:
THE 1966 ROYAL ALBERT HALL CONCERT

JOHN CALE
MERCY

ANIMAL COLLECTIVE
ISN'T IT NOW?

THE KILLS
GOD GAMES

TIRZAH
TRIP9LOVE...???

GEORGIA
EUPHORIC

PANDA BEAR & SONIC BOOM
RESET IN DUB

THE FOLK IMPLOSION
MUSIC FOR KIDS

PROTOMARTYR
FORMAL GROWTH IN THE DESERT

THE ART OF THE RUSE

IN 2006, A HISTORY OF FUNERARY MUSICIANS WAS PUBLISHED AND THEN QUICKLY
EXPOSED AS A HOAX. WHO WAS BEHIND IT, AND WHY?

by Fernando A. Flores

I n 1540, Henry the VIII ordered Thomas Cromwell to lure six musicians from Italy for the sole purpose of improving the court's music. They made it to Canterbury, where the jailer Joseph Babcotte, unaware of the king's plan, confiscated their instruments: six viols, two violins, two violas, and a violoncello. Two of the men died in captivity, and their violins went missing. The four survivors eventually left England with their instruments. Only one of them returned, finally reaching the king's court.

In 1566, the jailer's son, George Babcotte, at age twenty-four, made his first reported appearance playing the violin, accompanying a translated Ludovico Ariosto play at a carnival in London's exclusive Gray's Inn. Had he been inspired by his father's captives? "His playing was truly the saddest sound I have ever heard," John Lyly observed in a letter to Edward de Vere, the man some doubters credit as being the "real" author of Shakespeare's works. "It moved the whole of the crowd to tears repeatedly." With the ascension of Queen Elizabeth I to the crown in 1558, all prayers and Catholic rituals during funeral services were discouraged, making way for a Protestant overhaul, which enforced a strict code of conduct for each class of procession. In 1584, a "funerary violinist" was officially added to the heralds of the College of Arms to play at the burial of anyone with the status of baron or above. Babcotte thus became

the first public face of this mysterious and maligned subgenre of music.

I'm a sucker for weird anthologies that showcase niche art movements, and over the years I've amassed a small library, both on audio and on paper. Some vinyl finds include *Remolino de Oro: Coastal Cumbias from Colombia's Discos Fuentes 1961–1973* and *La Contra Ola: Synth Wave and Post Punk from Spain, 1980–86*. On the books side, I've spent hours immersed in *Imaginary Numbers: An Anthology of Marvelous Mathematical Stories, Diversions, Poems, and Musings*, which includes Christian Bök's unusual "Enantiomorphosis (A Natural History of Mirrors)," with partly mirrored text; and *100 Artists' Manifestos: From the Futurists to the Stuckists*, which contains Werner Herzog's 1999 "Minnesota Declaration," arguing for the use of "ecstatic truth" in documentary cinema—a state that can "be reached only through fabrication and imagination and stylization."

During the early COVID days of 2020, after losing my bookselling job and the routine I'd depended on, I escaped into such musical and textual compendiums as a distraction from reality. My discovery of Babcotte père et fils is thanks to a 2013 release from the enigmatic Mississippi Records label, titled *The Art of Funerary Violin: Contemporary Recordings by Members of the Guild of Funerary Violinists Under the Direction of Rohan Kriwaczek*. The album stayed on my turntable for weeks at a stretch. Its minimalist cover depicts a robed skeleton holding two femurs like a bow and violin, while the gothic solo pieces within, with occasional minimalist bass drum, seemed tailor-made for the inescapable pandemic deaths of the time.

The liner notes credit various eighteenth- and nineteenth-century composers, including Hieronymous Gratchenfleiss of Lower Saxony, the French master Pierre Dubuisson, and Charles Sudbury, England's "dark genius." I became fascinated with this genre I'd never heard of, and soon discovered there was a companion volume to the record, conveniently written by the musical director himself: Rohan Kriwaczek. The book was out of print, but I found it easily online. As I became preoccupied with the basic survival that year required, the handsome hardcover sat on my shelves practically untouched.

While downsizing my record collection recently, I came upon *The Art of Funerary Violin* once again. Its intensity had gone dormant for a few years as I figured out my finances; I eventually got my bookselling job back, and life returned to something like normal. To my relief, the ethereal music still soothed my spirit, bringing to mind imagery such as Virgil guiding lost souls through an unforgiving afterlife. I pulled the book—*An Incomplete History of the Art of Funerary Violin*—down from my crowded shelves, and approached it with renewed curiosity. I learned that funerary violin began as an improvised tradition, and the earliest written composition was a short suite in 1670. The Great Fire of London in 1666 destroyed most of the guild's early records. The biggest loss came during the Great Funerary Purges of 1833, when the Catholic Church confiscated or destroyed any surviving records and compositions held by the guild. (A faction in the Vatican that opposed exploitation through grief had bested its weaker rival.)

George Babcotte, the guild's founder and for a time its lone member, took his own life in 1607, while fleeing from an arrest warrant after being labeled a heretic. He was buried with a stake through his heart at an unremarkable Sussex crossroads. According to the book, most violinists associated with the guild died tragically, and little is known of them. (The Church was surprisingly thorough in its suppression.) The only member with anything like a modern photograph happens to be the author, Rohan Kriwaczek—the person also credited with assembling the Mississippi Records release.

Kriwaczek gives a brief history of funerary music, which he claims goes back thousands of years, and supplies capsule biographies of prominent members of the Guild of Funerary Violinists. Regarding his first encounter with the guild, he writes, "A more dreary collection of fellows could not be imagined, by me at least, although Dickens did at times come close." Engravings, photographs, and illustrations add dimension to the depictions of these unusual artists and events. One grows accustomed to the author's vague phrasing sprinkled among grandiose historical claims: "How he came to take on this role is unknown, but many scholars have suggested," he tells us, before speculating on Babcotte's undocumented rise to fame. After reading that Babcotte was the original inspiration behind the character of Hortensio in Shakespeare's *The Taming of the Shrew*, I was compelled to learn more about this violinist and the guild.

In October 2006, just weeks prior to the book's joint publication by Overlook Press in the States and Duckworth Books in the UK, *The New York Times* published an article revealing Kriwaczek's project as a hoax. Even the "funerary duels" that took France by storm in the early nineteenth century, where each violinist improvised around a melody (the one who drew the most tears was named the winner), were dismissed by historians and music experts as false. Peter Mayer, the publisher of Overlook, had acquired the manuscript as a nonfiction title for his list at the Frankfurt Book Fair the previous year, after being swept away by its claims. "It reads so extraordinarily serious and passionate," he told the *Times*.

Unlike literary hoaxes such as Clifford Irving's fake autobiography of Howard Hughes, the constructed literary persona JT LeRoy, or H. G. Carrillo's bogus Cuban identity, Rohan's project went beyond inventing a sole persona.

More audaciously, he added an entire footnote to the past five hundred years of musical history. "I just thought, whether it is true or not true, it is the work of some sort of crazy genius," Mayer told the *Times*. "If it is a hoax, it is a brilliant, brilliant hoax." (Mayer died in 2018.)

It's hard for me to reconcile this sublime music, which came to me during a difficult period in my life, with this bizarre invented history, just as I'm sure it was hard for Mayer to accept that the manuscript he'd published was a sham. A human being, after all, wrote the words that eventually became a book, researched the "real" history running alongside its fiction, and packaged this prank with elaborate graphics. The album was released six years after the book's publication; one wonders if Peter Mayer ever listened to the compositions. (Sheet music for the LP forms the appendix to the Overlook edition.)

Numerous emails to Overlook Press and Mississippi Records went unanswered, but after I tried several different addresses for Rohan Kriwaczek, he finally wrote back. His Overlook biography states that he graduated from the Royal Academy of Music in 1974; Rohan revealed to me that he was actually born in 1968, in London. He began composing on woodwinds at the age of eight, and took up Bulgarian bagpipes soon after, but in later years found the instrument unwieldy for his purposes as a travelling musician. It was after a snowstorm in Scotland in 1994, Rohan says, that he picked up the violin, which he taught himself by busking six hours a day. After five years, he says, he got "pretty good." The project began, "as me writing a bunch of solo violin music—something nobody was interested in.

I decided that rather than writing individual pieces, what I wanted to create was a genre, and a genre needs a history, and history needs good stories, heroes and villains, et cetera."

Rohan would get up at 6 a.m., research historical periods, search eBay for useful memorabilia, and "just wrote" the book. In his elaborate literary prank, he feels like a character from a Jorge Luis Borges story, yet he goes one step further by physically manifesting a piece of the impossible work described within the pages: the music on the record. "You have to understand," Rohan wrote to me, "I am an artist and live in the worlds I create, so at the time I totally believed in funerary violin, and I was just writing it into existence."

Fernando Pessoa, the early twentieth-century Portuguese writer, employed about 136 heteronyms with detailed biographies throughout his writing life. About the neopagan poet Alberto Caeiro, one of his most prolific alter egos, he once wrote, "I thought I would play a trick… and invent a bucolic poet of a rather complicated kind," hinting that his genesis was a joke. In this, Rohan has more in common with Pessoa than with Borges or any other forebear. On the Mississippi release, each violinist, credited with titles like "The Sombre Coquetry of Death," has his own stylistic flair. The distinct tempo and mood of the processional by Hieronymous Gratchenfleiss distinguish it from one of Charles Sudbury's maddening dirges, just as a poem by "Alberto Caeiro" has a voice that yearns differently from those of "Ricardo Reis" or "Álvaro de Campos"—Pessoa's two other dominant heteronyms.

In trying to imagine Rohan's book as a fiction submission looking for a publisher, the necessity of presenting the work as historically factual becomes obvious. As fiction, it's nearly unclassifiable—unpublishable, even. Its comparative titles are daring but inaccessible works such as *The Temple of Iconoclasts*, Juan Rodolfo Wilcock's 1972 compendium of mad scientists, or the invented Byzantium-like society that rivals Rome in Jean d'Ormesson's *The Glory of the Empire*—all extremely difficult to find English translations of, circa 2006.

Since the Mississippi compilation, Rohan Kriwaczek says, he has recorded ten more albums in various styles that he has no plans to release, merely hinting at being the sole creator of and performer behind funerary music. He claims that violinists get in touch with him, looking for more funerary violin sheet music to perform than the Overlook book has to offer. There are now bands, he informs me, dedicated to the genre of funerary violin, playing his arrangements and even writing new material. I couldn't find any such bands, however. I wasn't able to verify any of these claims. And it was never clear whether the Babcotte story was true or not—Rohan didn't reveal what was fact or fiction in the book. But I want to believe all of it, if only as the deeper strata of "ecstatic truth" Herzog vehemently argued for.

Only 1,500 copies of *An Incomplete History* were printed. Upon its scandalous release, a spokesperson at Duckworth told the *Daily Mail* that it would become a collector's item. On Spotify, there's solo violin music under Rohan's name, as well as plenty of tracks from the Guild of Funerary Violinists—at times, certain pieces overlap. Rohan Kriwaczek's elaborate twenty-first-century prank is a unique convergence of performance art, music, and literature to rival that of one of Borges's most famous characters, Pierre Menard, who attempted his own near-verbatim version of *Don Quixote*. But when was the last time you saw Menard's *Don Quixote* for sale anywhere? ✶

MICROINTERVIEW WITH VICTOR OLADIPO, PART I

THE BELIEVER: You recently released your third album, *TUNDE*, which explores your Nigerian heritage through Afrobeats. I can't think of any other NBA player who can sing—like actually *sing* sing—the way you do. Where did you get it from?

VICTOR OLADIPO: I started singing when I was small. My family was very religious. A go-to-church-every-Sunday-type family. I wasn't forced to sing, but I was always curious about joining the choir. I started singing in the church around the second or third grade. Before you knew it, I was leading the choir. Eight, nine years old. In high school, I tried out for the school chorus and I was so good that the teacher asked me to do that instead of basketball. I decided to quit chorus the next day because I didn't want it to interfere with my basketball. But yeah, man, a few of my cousins sing and play instruments. I have a cousin in the opera. I have an uncle who sings. We're a music-oriented family. My talent isn't super unique, but maybe it's unique to be able to do both at a high level. ✶

SOUND

FOGHORN

by Benjamin Anastas

FEATURES:

✶ Does not resemble anything human

✶ Soothing

✶ Barely attenuated by fog

My friend Buff was the first person I knew who had a Sony Walkman. Or it could have been another friend who brought the Walkman over to Buff's house in the summer of 1981; all I know for sure is that I listened to one for the first time in Buff's living room in Maine. From the window seat, I watched the others fiddle with the buttons, press EJECT and flip the cassette to the other side, weigh the body of the Walkman in their hands, and say, "Holy shit!" But the sound: that was the thing. When my turn came—the windows behind me white with fog, the logs in the fireplace hissing behind a hearth screen—I slid the headphones on while Buff pressed REWIND. It was Brian Eno's *Before and After Science* in the cassette slot. Buff rewound with clairvoyant accuracy to "King's Lead Hat," a song he believed in with a manic devotion that I could never share.

Buff must have subjected us to "King's Lead Hat" a hundred times that summer, extolling the jerky, discordant majesty of its unfolding, the relentless, mad pounding of the piano and drums. To me, it sounded like Roxy Music (Eno's former band) after a group-wide session of electroshock therapy. No: "King's Lead Hat" sounded like Roxy Music *during* a group-wide session of electroshock therapy. But when Buff pressed PLAY, and the song's fade-in was complete, I felt closer to its sonic disturbance than I ever had before. With the Walkman on, the sound enveloped me.

This all took place on an island in Downeast Maine, in the eerie isolation of the kind of fog the adults referred to as "pea soup." Buff's house, with its bank of picture

windows and clean modernist simplicity, felt like a lighthouse, the cove and stone beach below gone blank, and more fog crawling up the slope and through the stunted spruce trees and rugosa roses that bordered his front yard. The chill a fogbank brings is not just a matter of the temperature; it's the loss of any sense of direction in the world, the shock of facing a mirror that has suddenly emptied. I'm on the same island now, as I write this, looking out over silver sliding water to a shape I know instinctively as Great Duck Island, the horizon blurry with fog, a little school of mackerel making the water boil off the closest ledge. A seal looks on impassively, bald head swimming just above the surface, until it dives. Who knows what bloody drama happens underneath.

In June of 1959, my grandfather Franz, an acoustic engineer at the firm Bolt Beranek and Newman in Cambridge, Massachusetts, conducted a series of experiments at the lighthouse station on Great Duck Island for the US Coast Guard. He was an émigré from Jewish Prague, tense and obsessive, with no talent for or interest in bonding with his American coworkers. In 1938 he'd boarded a plane to attend a conference in London with the family jewels sewn into the lining of his jacket, and he spent the rest of his life as if pursued. Franz and the team he'd assembled were trying to measure how the thick fog endemic to that part of Maine attenuated the signal of the foghorn. Great Duck Island was encased in dense fog for a mean of forty to fifty days a year, according to a paper Franz later published in an industry journal—some years, staying on the island, it felt like we were fogged in for forty or fifty days a summer—and the old bull-roarer foghorn at the lighthouse station produced the same booming wail every time it sounded, making it ideal for taking measurements. They erected loudspeakers on the shore emitting random noise in one-third octave frequency bands (basically

Illustration by Andrea Settimo

the constituent frequencies of any sound we hear), and outfitted a fifty-six-foot Coast Guard vessel with sound-receiving equipment: two microphones with windscreens and a battery-operated tape recorder in the cabin with an acoustic calibrator that would activate the recorder when signals were detected.

Here is the thing that amazes me: my grandfather and his team constructed micrometeorological equipment to measure wind and temperature gradients on the water, and a "miniature wind tunnel" that allowed them to capture and measure the size of the water droplets in the fog. I didn't know that wind tunnels came in miniature sizes, or that fog could be measured with that degree of precision, at least not in 1959. Then they set out in their Mad Scientist Fog and Foghorn Distillation Craft and followed a prelaid course of marker buoys four thousand yards to the south of the lighthouse, taking measurements with their homemade equipment at intervals along the way. When that was done, they started all over again and took measurements along another four-thousand-yard course of marker buoys to the northeast. I didn't think too much about the two courses of marker buoys when I read the paper for the first time, but then it dawned on me: four thousand yards is nearly two miles of open sea. In the pea soup, with the foghorn groaning its signal in the distance—a "throat," as W. S. Merwin puts it in his poem "Foghorn," that "does not call to anything human."

The paper itself is a kind of anticlimax. Figures and graphs show the results of various measurements: the foghorn signal itself over ocean water, and in different types of fog, and the attenuation in the signals of the random noise generator. But in his conclusion, my grandfather writes that "sound attenuation by typical sea fogs… along the eastern seaboard of the United States is small (<1 db / 1000 yd)." Absent any fog, the sound attenuation over ocean water is essentially the same. Fog has virtually no effect on the way the sound of the foghorn travels.

I didn't know about my grandfather's experiments on Great Duck Island when I spent summers with the staging area in clear view. I saw two long humps of forest stretched out until they were taut, a stony meadow with a landing strip for small planes holding them in balance. Way out on the island's point, the lighthouse and the buildings of the Coast Guard station looked no bigger than tremors on an Etch A Sketch. The foghorn was omnipresent, a soothing voice through the walls of my grandfather's house at night—my dead grandfather, who might as well have still been out on his fifty-six-foot craft measuring fog droplets. Did he feel more at home out on the water, making calculations at every marker buoy, than he normally did in a country that he couldn't understand?

I think of the magnetic tape machine running in the cabin of the boat, clicking on and off with the arrival of every signal along the course of nighttime buoys, and recording—what? "King's Lead Hat," maybe. Or a sound so tedious, untenable, and strange that even Buff would have spared us from listening to it on his Walkman.

Those tape reels from the cabin of the boat. That is the music of the fog in Maine. That is what it must sound like to be lost at sea. ✶

EVERY KNOWN COLLEGE OFFERING A TAYLOR SWIFT– INSPIRED COURSE

✶ New York University: Swiftology 101
✶ Arizona State University: Psychology of Taylor Swift
✶ Stanford University: All Too Well (Ten Week Version) and The Last Great American Songwriter: Storytelling with Taylor Swift Through the Eras
✶ Berklee College of Music: Songs of Taylor Swift
✶ Queen's University: Taylor Swift's Literary Legacy
✶ St. Thomas University: Communications and Taylor Swift
✶ The University of Texas at Austin: The Taylor Swift Songbook
✶ University of Missouri: Taylor Swiftory: History and Literature Through Taylor Swift
✶ Binghamton University: Taylor Swift, 21C Music
✶ Ghent University: Literature: Taylor's Version
✶ Queen Mary University of London: Taylor Swift and Literature
✶ Rice University: Miss Americana: The Evolution and Lyrics of Taylor Swift
✶ University of Kansas: The Sociology of Taylor Swift
—list compiled by Emily Lang

HAUSER & WIRTH PUBLISHERS

URSULA GOES TO PARIS
WITH TAKESADA MATSUTANI

With an exclusive poster by Henry Taylor

Plus Camille Henrot, Marie Baléo, Kathy Acker, Stanley Greene and more

ISSUE 9
NOW AVAILABLE

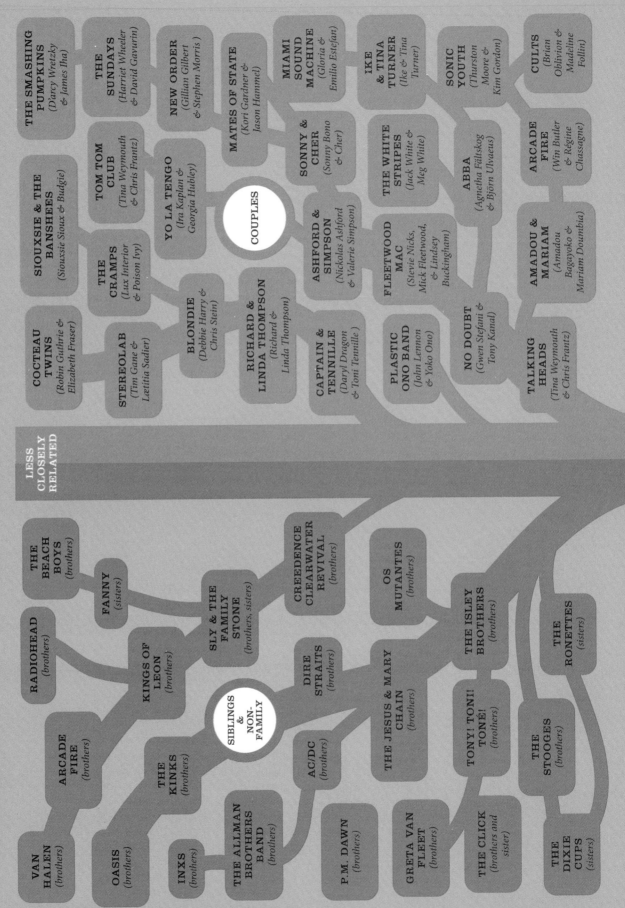

FAMILY BAND FAMILY TREE

THE 100% NATURAL GOOD-TIME

COUPLES

THE SMASHING PUMPKINS *(Darcy Wretzky & James Iha)*

THE SUNDAYS *(Harriet Wheeler & David Gavurin)*

NEW ORDER *(Gillian Gilbert & Stephen Morris)*

MATES OF STATE *(Kori Gardner & Jason Hammel)*

MIAMI SOUND MACHINE *(Gloria & Emilio Estefan)*

IKE & TINA TURNER *(Ike & Tina Turner)*

SONIC YOUTH *(Thurston Moore & Kim Gordon)*

CULTS *(Brian Oblivion & Madeline Follin)*

SIOUXSIE & THE BANSHEES *(Siouxsie Sioux & Budgie)*

TOM TOM CLUB *(Tina Weymouth & Chris Frantz)*

YO LA TENGO *(Ira Kaplan & Georgia Hubley)*

SONNY & CHER *(Sonny Bono & Cher)*

THE WHITE STRIPES *(Jack White & Meg White)*

ABBA *(Agnetha Fältskog & Björn Ulvaeus)*

ARCADE FIRE *(Win Butler & Régine Chassagne)*

COCTEAU TWINS *(Robin Guthrie & Elizabeth Fraser)*

THE CRAMPS *(Lux Interior & Poison Ivy)*

STEREOLAB *(Tim Gane & Letitia Sadier)*

BLONDIE *(Debbie Harry & Chris Stein)*

RICHARD & LINDA THOMPSON *(Richard & Linda Thompson)*

ASHFORD & SIMPSON *(Nickolas Ashford & Valerie Simpson)*

FLEETWOOD MAC *(Stevie Nicks, Mick Fleetwood, & Lindsey Buckingham)*

AMADOU & MARIAM *(Amadou Bagayoko & Mariam Doumbia)*

CAPTAIN & TENNILLE *(Daryl Dragon & Toni Tennille)*

PLASTIC ONO BAND *(John Lennon & Yoko Ono)*

NO DOUBT *(Gwen Stefani & Tony Kanal)*

TALKING HEADS *(Tina Weymouth & Chris Frantz)*

LESS CLOSELY RELATED

SIBLINGS & NON-FAMILY

THE BEACH BOYS *(brothers)*

RADIOHEAD *(brothers)*

FANNY *(sisters)*

KINGS OF LEON *(brothers)*

SLY & THE FAMILY STONE *(brothers, sisters)*

CREEDENCE CLEARWATER REVIVAL *(brothers)*

OS MUTANTES *(brothers)*

THE KINKS *(brothers)*

ARCADE FIRE *(brothers)*

VAN HALEN *(brothers)*

OASIS *(brothers)*

INXS *(brothers)*

THE ALLMAN BROTHERS BAND *(brothers)*

DIRE STRAITS *(brothers)*

AC/DC *(brothers)*

THE JESUS & MARY CHAIN *(brothers)*

THE ISLEY BROTHERS *(brothers)*

TONY! TONI! TONE! *(brothers)*

THE RONETTES *(sisters)*

THE STOOGES *(brothers)*

P.M. DAWN *(brothers)*

GRETA VAN FLEET *(brothers)*

THE CLICK *(brothers and sister)*

THE DIXIE CUPS *(sisters)*

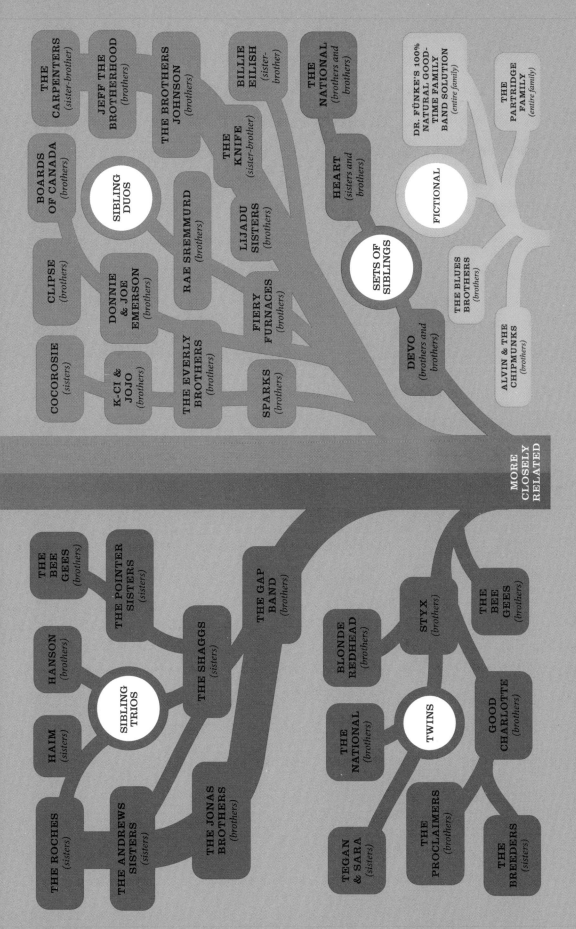

The term *dynamic range* describes the difference in decibels between the quietest and the loudest sounds in a mix. Of course, maybe a more familiar sense of *dynamic* has to do with the ways we relate to one another—our interpersonal gravities. Of all human enterprises, families and bands have got to be the most intense. Where else do you find such levels of care, safety, home, belonging—and also anger, treachery, and betrayal? Overlay these two dynamics, and the potential for dissonance is basically unfathomable. There is something so intense about the idea of combining the hectic crucible of family life with the no less (or possibly more?) hectic crucible of band life that is—as a cultural object—irresistible. Considering the family band feels a bit like rubbernecking at simultaneous train wrecks. The energy radiated by the ultra-dynamic social-sonic firework of their collision is bewildering and bedazzling all at once. —*Justin Carder and Sunra Thompson*

THE PROCESS

IN WHICH AN ARTIST DISCUSSES MAKING A PARTICULAR WORK

Lol Tolhurst, *Goth: A History*, 2023

A month before my father officiated my marriage on a cliffside in Bolinas, California, my parents took me shopping for a wedding shirt in San Francisco. While we were browsing in a boutique in Pacific Heights, deciding between gray and blue, "Just Like Heaven" by the Cure began playing through the store speakers.

"Do you know this song, Dad?" I joked. He looked back inquisitively, unable to discern the low-volume melody with his percussion-damaged hearing. Behind us, the salesperson said to her coworker, "This is definitely one of my top ten favorite songs."

"Does the Cure still tour?" her coworker asked.

"I'm not sure. They're hella old now."

We all know this song. We hear it in Ubers and elevators, grocery stores and train stations, on first dates and during heartbreaks, at bat mitzvahs and weddings. It is, by all definitions of the word, a hit. Unbeknownst to the girls behind the register, I know this song, too, because my dad helped write it.

Meanwhile, in the boutique, my father, blissfully out of earshot, handed me a shirt to try on; the clerk tapped her fingers to the sound of my dad playing keyboards in 1987. This shadow of influence—the work of artistic forebears—weighs heavily on the minds of aspiring artists. In my case, this anxiety is two-fold in the sense that my flesh-and-blood patriarch is also my artistic forebear. Early in my career, I distanced myself from his scope of influence by a refusal of proximity. I learned guitar,

Photo by Louis Rodiger

but never drums or keyboard; went to graduate school for creative writing instead of touring with my band; and published poems instead of songs. I tried my best to distance myself and my work from what he had done, in pursuit of something he had no jurisdiction over, something that wouldn't elicit comparison, where my last name didn't matter.

If my father has taught me anything, it's that avoidance breeds suffering, and in my early twenties, while I tried to focus on making chapbooks and finishing my MFA, I found myself playing in rock groups almost by accident, and eventually formed my own group, Topographies. As if by osmosis, the echoes of my father's record collection pedagogy in my early years were in Topographies' music—Joy Division, Can, the Fall. At the dinner table when I was growing up, we discussed the fact that Interpol borrowed from Joy Division (but more from the Chameleons). I was read Camus before bedtime. I was ten years old, and I didn't know these were gifts: an upbringing in which art-making was regarded as a serious and reasonable life choice, and being given the knowledge that no one can escape the weight of the great artists who came before them. I, like most artists, am both buoyed and haunted by the artists I admire. But I hold the unique privilege that one of those specters of music history is often in my apartment for a weekend visit, playing with my dog on the air mattress, trying to find a vegan lunch option.

When my father first approached me about a possible collaboration, about doing the research for his book Goth: A History, which traces goth from its eighteenth-century literary roots to its flourishing as a subculture, I could sense in our conversation a mutual reticence. We love all the same things, but have never had much success in collaboration. Once, on a weekend trip to the Northern California coast, we tried making music together, but did so with such trepidation and caution around each other that we produced something unlistenable and resorted to hiking instead. However, after some deliberation, I agreed to be his researcher for this project because I realized that working together on this book was markedly different: we weren't trying to create something new but were continuing a conversation we'd already been having my entire life. Like building a deck or fixing a car, working on Goth: A History became the intermediary for a deeper experience of connection between us, not only as father and son but as two artists with deep admiration for each other.

—Gray Tolhurst

THE BELIEVER: Why did you want to write a book about the history of goth?

LOL TOLHURST: For me, this book was a chance to expand my writing capability. The first book I wrote, Cured [: The Tale of Two Imaginary Boys], was a memoir, and that was terrifying. But it was easy to write, because all I had to do was remember things and pull out the things that were interesting about those experiences and then figure out, well, if it's interesting to me, will it be interesting to somebody else? But this book was a whole different beast. You know: Why write a book about goth culture? Does anybody really care? I mean, other than other goths? I wanted to do something that would make people care. I wanted to articulate how goths fit into the cultural framework. You helped me do that. You studied anthropology. I wanted this book to be a cultural anthropology of goth. Goth is not just entertainment—you know that. The movement was about how to understand what the hell was going on with me, with everything. Goth was the way I understood the world.

BLVR: Yes, I totally agree. Goth is a countercultural movement. Goth: A History is tracing the continued history of that counterculture. It's interesting to try to contextualize something so unwieldy as an entire movement in a single book, especially a movement like goth that is still living and evolving. When I read nonfiction, I always ask myself, What value does this perspective have? You know, like: What value does the perspective of this specific researcher, this specific journalist, have? I think there's an implicit value to you being the author of Goth: A History because you were there at the origins of the movement, and you've done so much to shape the musical and cultural aesthetic.

LT: Well, I can look very clearly and succinctly at the times when it was going on, the times when I was involved with it, and I do have a point of view about that. So that gives me the right to write about it, I guess. I mean, it doesn't mean that I have the final word by any means, but that really wasn't what I wanted to do, anyway. I wanted to write about where goth came from. I wanted to open a discussion.

BLVR: You wanted to expand the dialogue. You're not trying to delineate. I mean, the way I view the book is that it's not a project of defining or cataloging goth. That is the role of the archivist or the art historian or whatever, to codify and partition everything into little boxes.

LT: I always hated the idea that everything has to be categorized into a little box.

BLVR: Nobody wants to pigeonhole themselves into a single movement. But if you had to define it, what is goth?

LT: I believe the word *goth* was originally used to describe medieval churches where the central architectural feature was the windows that would let in light. I like this origin of the word because it seems like an accurate description of what goth music is doing too. Goth music lets the light in. I know goth music is associated with darkness, but I actually really do associate it with light. The best goth music illuminates the darkest corners of us. Goth is not somebody wearing bats on their head or, you know, sleeping in a casket. It's a way of looking at things and perceiving the world.

BLVR: Would you say that it's more of a philosophy than an aesthetic?

LT: Yes, it's more of a philosophy because it is similar to the ethos of punk. I mean, one of the things goth got from punk was the do-it-yourself attitude, and the notion that you could actually be whoever you wanted to be. Back in the day, at the Batcave, not everybody dressed like what we perceive now as goth. There were some very, very normal-looking people, and some very outrageous-looking people, as well. You could be a little geeky, you could be a little strange, but you didn't have to have all the right clothes to be accepted. Everybody was welcome. It's much more of a philosophical standpoint than an aesthetic standpoint.

BLVR: Things like goth and punk get filtered into the culture as aesthetics of mainstream fashion. It's their most visible aspect, and also their most consumable aspect. But it's interesting that at the Batcave there weren't tons of people that were visibly goth, because the aesthetic of goth was still in development. What do you think about the recognized goth aesthetic?

LT: You know this because you lived with me through your formative years. I subscribe to some aspects of the goth aesthetic. I don't own many clothes that are not monochromatic. But I also feel that, like punk, goth has an aesthetic freedom and can encompass lots of different things. I think it was a natural progression that the aesthetic of goth, which was post-punk, was darker and gloomier than punk. You have to think of where it came from. Goth came from the end of the '70s in England, which was pretty grim in lots of ways. It fit the national mood, especially in England. Goth is also less nihilistic and more serious and sensual than punk was.

BLVR: Would you say the aesthetic of goth is related to the political and social circumstance of late-'70s England?

LT: Absolutely. It came out of that culture and that history. The thing that drew me in and made it something I wanted to explore was the fact that it had more emotions in it than the straight nihilism of punk. Punk was really about kicking down the doors and destroying everything, and, you know, that didn't last long, because obviously at some point you've got to have something to do. The postwar world naturally transitioned from punk to goth. I loved goth. It gave me a reason to be sad, but it also gave me a reason to be happy.

BLVR: It's easy to subdivide and categorize this music, this fashion, this art, within the timeline of cultural history and art history. But when you're in something like that, when you're part of the movement, I imagine it's harder to discern.

LT: Yes, absolutely. It is. It's really unknown to you when you're in the thick of it, because you're living it. You're not analyzing. That's why it was good for me to wait until this point in my life to write about some things that happened forty years ago. Without that distance, I don't think I could have made a correct analysis of it. I couldn't have understood it.

BLVR: I also question how much dialogue there was at the time about this being a new thing or if people just thought of it as rock and roll.

LT: No, I definitely think people thought of it as something different. I know that's true because that change had come a little earlier, in '77, '76, with the punk movement. We definitely considered ourselves to be apart from rock and roll, even though, as you know, many years later, looking back, we saw we were influenced by certain aspects of what came before us. It was sort of de rigueur at the time to pretend the world didn't exist before 1976. But, of course, the world did exist before 1976. Goth could not have existed without punk.

BLVR: When the Cure was making music, who were you thinking of as your forebears?

LT: There's a psychedelic feel about a lot of the things we made. But it was in a less blues-based kind of way, I think. We came into it more out of the three chords and the truth-telling of punk. If I look at bands that came before us, like Can, for instance, they sounded technically quite competent and equally technically incompetent. And that's actually what made them good. I mean, I loved drummers like Jaki Liebezeit because he was very brilliant at what he was doing. But it wasn't of the time either. It was a different style. And he wanted to create a different style, to be something different. What's his famous phrase? I think he said: "You must play monotonous." And I understood that, because that's where I wanted to go. I didn't want to fill out the drums with a lot of different fills. And even though I listened to people like Billy Cobham and others who were very intricate drummers, that wasn't who I saw myself as then. I saw myself as pushing things in a more minimal way. That minimalism really started with *Seventeen Seconds*. We thought of ourselves as being experimental, not like the next thing after Gene Vincent. I look at myself playing and I know I got some things from Ringo. I see where I get the hi-hat from him and Charlie Watts. So there are things that came down the line. I can't deny they did. There was a time when we naively thought we had escaped the past. I don't think you can escape the past.

BLVR: All the people you name—like Ringo, Charlie Watts—none of those people are particularly goth. Would you agree?

LT: They weren't goth, but I felt they had a germ of it. It's not even originality; it's that they believed in what they were doing. They were genuine. And that's what I was looking for. I was looking for something that was genuine, that felt good to me.

BLVR: What was it like working with me, your son, as a researcher and collaborator on this book project?

LT: There are fewer opportunities in the modern world to work with your children, or with your parents, than there used to be. Pre–Industrial Revolution, that used to be the thing—you were destined to do what your father or mother did, and that was who you were. The world works differently now, and that's probably for the best, but I valued and enjoyed the time I spent working with you as your equal, as a fellow artist. It's exciting for me to engage with somebody I love on that level. Some fathers and sons work stuff out on the golf course or at the basketball hoop or something. But I think it was important for us to find that connection in this book. It was mystical and wonderful. Can I flip the tables? How was it for you?

BLVR: It was challenging for me to work on this book with you, because I think I have this natural desire to want to do better than you. I had to transcend that. There was bound to be some tension because we work in the same fields and are interested in the same things. I'll admit there was a period, when we were working on the book, when I wanted to beat you.

LT: Like physically beat me with the book? [*Laughs*]

BLVR: No. I wanted to best you in it.

LT: You wanted to have your own thing.

BLVR: Prose writing was a wonderful medium to collaborate in because it's something we both do, but at same time it's not our primary medium.

LT: It's more of a primary medium for you because you've been trained in it. You were able to put together the research for *Goth: A History* in a way I could not do.

BLVR: Well, that's because you didn't go to an American college. I did attend a graduate writing program, but in many ways writing can't be taught. By collaborating on this book project, I think, we were able to take our egos out of it. It helped that the book was a history of goth music. It's not a transcription of your life. The book is about the movement that you helped found and shape, but it's one step removed from you. It wasn't like giving you my song or something, or vice versa, and us trying to cocreate an entirely new piece of art together. I think cocreating at that level is difficult with any other person, really.

LT: As your father, I always wanted, and I still always want, for you to just be doing the things you are good at. I want you to eclipse me. And that's not because I'm not proud of what I've done. I didn't have this kind of relationship with my father, because I wasn't in awe of him. I'm not saying you're in awe of me. I wanted to be better than my father too. Sure. But I didn't want to be better than him at what he would have thought was better than him. He was a very damaged person in lots of ways, so the last thing I wanted to do was imitate his path. I didn't want to be him. I didn't want to go into the navy. I didn't want to be the kind of person that he became in the latter part of his life. I didn't want to be as unhappy as he was.

BLVR: Yeah. I mean, even though I think of your life and what you do as cool, I still do not want to be you.

LT: No, of course not. I want you to be self-actualized, which is one of the reasons I never went out at the very beginning, calling up all the managers I knew, and all the people I knew, for you. I wasn't going to do any of that, because that is unnecessary for you, because you are strong enough. I'm in awe of the way you go about some things. When I came to see you recently, you had a hundred pieces of music you were working on—I'm in awe of somebody that can be so purposeful about composition. Composition is happenstance to me. I don't have a method. You seem to be building on your

method all the time, which is awesome, because I don't have that facility.

BLVR: What is your creative life like?

LT: My life has been in three distinct periods. There was the period before you were born, the period when you were born up until the day you left home, and then this later time we're in now, in which things seem to have come back in a way where I can make things again, because for a long time I was making stuff, but it was very small and minuscule, because the thing I really wanted to do was to be your dad.

BLVR: This can really spiral into a whole different conversation about art-making and child-rearing that I am fascinated by, but I think that will take up too much space in this interview.

LT: I'm quite happy to have white hair and to be this age and to be a little saggy. I'm enjoying this part of my life because I get to enjoy conversations with you as a man and as an artist. The fact that you're my son is just an added bonus. This closeness is not an experience that my father—your grandfather—and I ever had. I feel very sorry for him that he didn't have it, because I know it must have made him feel very, very sad and lonely. And I know that won't be the case for you and me. I think the whole striving thing is a good thing. It helps me up my game. It helps you up your game. As long as it's not done in an oedipal flurry of nonsense. Obviously, I'm

---

MICROINTERVIEW WITH VICTOR OLADIPO, PART II

THE BELIEVER: What influence have your parents had on your music?

VICTOR OLADIPO: My dad always played music in the car. My mom too. Always to and from school, church. Honestly, I think the whole world engages with music in some fashion. There's so many songs, a song for everything. I think everyone has music in their life. My mom introduced me to Marvin Gaye, Aretha Franklin, Lionel Richie. That kind of stuff. It's what I heard growing up. It was hard not to get into it. ✴

coming from the aspect of fatherhood, but I can't come from any other aspect. I can't come from your aspect, because I didn't feel close to my father. I didn't know him well. He was not available to me emotionally. I hope I am available to you emotionally.

BLVR: You are. Do you think you can be a practicing artist and a father simultaneously? Do you think being a father and having that experience has fundamentally changed your practice as an artist?

LT: The answer to both those questions is yes. I feel fatherhood was the greatest stimulus in my artistic life, because instead of being constantly mono-focused on my feelings and my emotions and my tribulations, fatherhood forces you to experience life through the eyes of another that you love and care for. I tend to think that everybody is all one thing, and I thought that for a long time, but I *really* thought it once I became a father, because I realized all I'm seeing is a reflection of myself, a reflection of who I am and who I could be and all those things. Pre-parenthood is like only seeing things in 2-D—it's like the medieval period before painters discovered perspective. The older I get, the more I realize there has to be some kind of celestial plan, because everything fits together so succinctly the older you get, and you realize, Oh, that's why that was. Having you, having a child, was a very good bridge into other parts of myself that I never would have discovered otherwise. I know it's going to sound a bit hokey, but after you were born, I was no longer alone with my own thoughts. I had to involve somebody else's thoughts and feelings. It's been a different trip.

BLVR: Pretty psychedelic, man.

LT: [*Laughs*]

BLVR: I don't yet see the world as making so much sense. It's a sort of fragmented, primordial stage for me, even at thirty-one. I'm still not sure where it's all going. Through art and music, I'm trying to make sense of that fragmentation, but the meaning is very amorphous to me.

LT: Even though I see some things clearly now, there's always some stuff that's not clear. But the difference is that now I

don't care that it's not that clear. It's not that important to me for it to be clear. It's not important for me to understand the world completely. It's important for me to accept that it *is*.

BLVR: This is where I wanted the conversation to go. I wanted to go in this direction, expand outward and into these broader ideas about art-making. But I just want to wrap up with a few quick structural questions about the book. Who is the most goth band of all time?

LT: It has to be the one with my friend Kevin Haskins. It has to be Bauhaus.

BLVR: Because?

LT: Just because.

BLVR: [*Laughs*] OK, we're going to leave that in there! What was the most goth Cure album? You're going to say *Pornography*, probably?

LT: Yes, yes. And *Faith*. *Pornography* is more despairing, but hopeful. And I see *Faith* the other way round, more hopeful with a little despair in it. *Faith* is like tea and cakes with lace curtains, and *Pornography* is a Francis Bacon painting gone mad.

BLVR: I like those two very English references. What's the most goth Cure song? That's a little harder.

LT: "Cold." Yeah, but just the beginning. Because the beginning is just the most lurching slab of goth. I can still see Robert in the studio with the cello on his lap, playing it like a guitar with the bow for the beginning and then the drums—one of my favorite drum parts ever, you know, just lumbering in like a big tank or something.

BLVR: We've got less than a minute on Zoom, so I'm going to get off, but I think we have plenty of info.

LT: Oh, gosh, we got material for a great article.

BLVR: Yeah, thanks, Dad. I love you.

LT: I love you too. That's how we end it. I love you. ✶

PLAYING FROM THE KEEP

ON THE PECULIAR GENRE OF ELECTRONIC MUSIC THAT BECAME THE SOUNDTRACK FOR DUNGEONCRAWLS

by Stu Horvath

In the early nineties, bands like Mayhem and Darkthrone kicked off the second wave of black metal in Norway, flooding the senses with screeching vocals, blast-beat drums, and blazing tremolo. But there have always been moments of calm in the chaos: ambient instrumentals, often incorporating medieval compositions, acoustic guitars, woodwinds, and the occasional mournful female vocal melody. These sonic shelters let the listener catch a breath while priming them for ever more brutal riffage.

The interludes also allowed for experimentation with electronic instruments. The first seven albums by Mortiis (1993 through 1999), who often performs wearing goblin-like prosthetics and describes his work from this period as "dark dungeon music," are a prime example, as are the two science fiction–inflected Neptune Towers albums (1994, 1995), recorded by Fenriz of Darkthrone. By embracing synths, such bands tapped into modes explored by electronic pioneers like Tangerine Dream and Skinny Puppy. Just as important, they inspired a host of DIY enthusiasts, who distributed their recordings on limited runs of cassettes.

The result is moody, minimalist electronic music that verges on primitive. The notes echo and convey a sense of distance, while the drone constricts. Together, these instrumental crosscurrents evoke a sense of the cavernous: a vast space full of suffocating darkness.

Despite their spareness, these compositions manage to be psychologically punishing in large doses. Like a dungeon, I suppose.

For many years, this musical movement didn't have a name. It merely *existed*, truly underground, mostly sustained by the swapping of tapes and, once the aughts ushered in easy access to high-speed internet, through the downloading of obscurely named MP3s. It spread by word of mouth, like a sinister secret. In 2011, someone with the reversible handle Andrew Werdna started the *Dungeon Synth* blog to quantify the genre and chart its almost willfully obscure history. The name stuck. In 2012, Erang released *Tome I*, the first album intentionally recorded and released as "dungeonsynth."

Of course, every subculture has its lunatic fringe. This is particularly true of second-wave black metal, which was born out of church burnings, murder, and suicide. (In fact, while in prison in the nineties for murder and arson,

white-supremacist guitarist Varg Vikernes could make music only on a synth, which means he sometimes gets credit for being a dungeonsynth pioneer, but honestly, fuck that guy.) Because of its origins in black metal, dungeonsynth shares that scene's infestation by crypto-fascists and blood-and-soil nationalists. Vetting is further complicated by dungeonsynth's lack of lyrics and the tendency of its artists to work under pseudonyms. To my knowledge, unless otherwise noted, the recording artists I mention here don't seem to be Nazis, but listeners should still proceed with caution.

Anyway, once a genre is named, there are suddenly "rules" and conventions to be embraced or defied. Permutations proliferate, the river becomes a delta, and new gimmicks arise. For instance, dungeonsynth cross-pollinates with other styles of electronic music, mutating at every contact. Traditionalists stick to the more identifiable black metal sounds, with some going so far as to disqualify projects not connected in some way to established black metal acts. Others gravitate to the clear similarities dungeonsynth has to the music of early games. I've witnessed heated arguments over this, but honestly, I couldn't tell you the difference between, say, the music that came out of my Nintendo while playing *Shadowgate* in 1989 and most 16-bit-style albums, like Cauldron 80's (excellent) *Devourer*.

Illustration by Noah Van Sciver

At some point, dungeonsynth became aurally tied to tabletop role-playing games (RPGs). The first clear instance of crossover was probably Corvus Neblus's album *Chapter I—Strahd's Possession*, which was inspired by the Ravenloft campaign setting for Dungeons & Dragons and released on cassette in 1999. There's a natural overlap between the gothic spires and the creeping undead of the setting and the melancholy, echoing refrains of the music. The RPG connection gained critical mass around 2017, coinciding with an explosion of zine projects that has continued to reshape the RPG hobby. Mothership (2018), a space horror RPG in the mode of the film *Event Horizon* and the videogame *Dead Space*, crystallized the movement; now there are zines for every possible RPG experience, from investigating bizarre events as public access TV station personalities (*WHPA-13*) to hunting monsters in 1889 Japan (*Yokai Hunters Society*). As a homemade form of music, usually created by a single person and distributed online, dungeonsynth pairs perfectly with RPG creators, who are often lone wolves themselves.

There are hundreds of RPG-ready dungeonsynth artists out there. You could build a whole castle out of their names: Secret Stairways, the Vampire Tower, Sequestered Keep. I'm partial to the releases from the Milan-based Heimat der Katastrophe, a tape label that has released 144 titles since 2017. Its fantasy-tinged products often provide bespoke soundtracks for established RPGs like MÖRK BORG or adventure gamebooks like *Lone Wolf*. Heimat's large range of releases encourages further experimentation as well: albums

veer into synthwave and kosmische, providing music suitable for space stations, shadowy alleys, and dystopic cities as well as dungeons.

I recently discovered Out of Season, a label that puts out dungeonsynth and metal in a variety of formats, all arranged around the aesthetics of fantasy and roleplaying games. One artist, Oublieth, makes gloriously brooding songs, and has album covers illustrated by Stephen Fabian, whose somber drawings define the aforementioned Ravenloft setting. Meanwhile, Fogweaver's titles and album art draw directly from Ursula K. Le Guin's Earthsea, a six-book series that interrogates many of the fantasy genre's assumptions, particularly about gender roles. It's a welcome crossover for Le Guin, a literary voice that's underappreciated in the rosters of RPG inspirations.

On a shelf in my loft are sixteen cassettes stacked in shiny plastic cases, like gleaming trinkets from some alternate past, bearing names like Kobold and Loot the Body on their spines. The J-cards are luridly illustrated, mostly in black and white, in an amateurish style that evokes the art of early tabletop roleplaying games. The cover for the first Kobold album, *The Cave of the Lost Talisman* (2017), riffs on an illustration by Bob Maurus from the D&D module *Ghost of Lion Castle* (1984)—a view not unlike that of a first-person videogame, with one hand holding a torch, the other a sword, and a snarling kobold approaching. Later albums keep the same composition, but switch out the menacing monster: skeleton, ogre, mummy. The cassette inserts list characters and their attributes, along with dungeon maps and

brief descriptions of the perils found therein: a playable scenario.

The low-res music of Kobold and similar RPG-influenced projects, complete with the occasional clanking chain or dripping water effect for extra dankness, seem distinct from earlier dungeonsynth. The newer, game-inspired iterations are still crowding and claustrophobic, but also favor sharp tones that are nostalgic and surprisingly warm—I suspect that much of the music was composed on vintage Casio keyboards. The result is engrossing but oddly punishing, perhaps because the songs lack the cathartic aggro of black metal. Rather, they provide an atmospheric backdrop for play. These are soundscapes for rolling dice over, for creating those accidental, delicious moments when action in the session—a rogue opening a chest that might contain a poison needle trap, a bugbear pulling a player character into the shadows—melds with urgent crescendos. This is music with a specific job. It isn't for casual listening. At least I can't listen for very long, not in the same way I can to other instrumental music. It's the history too. Because it's tied to nihilistic wastoids in the same ways black metal can be, dungeonsynth requires careful exploration and a willingness to check every flagstone underfoot for snares.

It's exhausting work, and an air of fatigue lingers around even the good finds. Perhaps the slog of it all makes dungeonsynth true to its name. These *are* songs that are well suited for secret places underground, that are played to match your footsteps when you're hesitantly stalking down the torchlit corridors of your imagination. There are treasures to be had, but dangers too. ✶

RHIANNON GIDDENS

[MUSICIAN]

"I THINK THAT'S WHY AMERICAN MUSIC IS SO POPULAR:
EVERYBODY SEES A PIECE OF THEMSELVES IN IT. IT'S IMPORTANT
TO SAY WE'RE JUST A LINK IN A CHAIN."

Artistic paths not taken for Rhiannon Giddens, for varying reasons:
Opera diva
Nashville pop star
Broadway lead
"An interpreter in a gown with a big hanging microphone"

I spoke with Rhiannon Giddens in mid-June 2023, soon after the announcement that her opera, Omar, cowritten with composer Michael Abels, had won the Pulitzer Prize for Music. The award is just the most recent jewel in Giddens's crown; she's also won two Grammys, a MacArthur grant, a spot in the North Carolina Music Hall of Fame, and the Steve Martin Banjo Prize, among many other honors.

But these achievements only hint at the broader impact of Giddens's work over the last twenty years. Since debuting with the Carolina Chocolate Drops, an all-Black old-time music group featuring Dom Flemons and Justin Robinson, Giddens has arguably done more than any single musician to broaden the look and sound of the Americana scene. You can hear her influence in the growing number of prominent Black artists who play and sing country- and folk-oriented music, notably Amythyst Kiah, Allison Russell, and Leyla McCalla, who collaborated with Giddens in 2019 as the quartet Our Native Daughters.

Illustration by Kristian Hammerstad

Giddens's multicultural background (her father is white, her mother is Black, and she also has Native American heritage) lends her special insight into the polyglot origins of her music—and her country. Omar *tells the real-life story of an enslaved Muslim man in South Carolina, and Giddens's song-based albums similarly address grave historical events, from slave auctions to church bombings. She has an evangelical sense of purpose when speaking about the banjo, and a dire need to complicate the widespread preconception that it's simply a hillbilly guitar. In interviews, at educational concerts, and on television series like her current PBS show,* My Music, *Giddens has told the true story of the banjo, which originated in Africa and the Caribbean. To her, its evolution into a "country" signifier embodies America's intrinsically multiracial culture. This global, historical focus makes her a natural collaborator with Yo-Yo Ma, whom Giddens succeeded as artistic director of the Silkroad Ensemble.*

In August 2023, Giddens released You're the One, *her first album of all-original pop material, written in a variety of styles, from classic soul to lush balladry. In a shift from her earlier, more rustic-sounding records,* You're the One *was produced by Jack Splash, a collaborator with Kendrick Lamar and other pop stars. On the verge of beginning her biggest-ever tour, and having just won a major award for composition, Giddens in 2023 is emblematic of the changing, expanding nature of Americana music today: there are more Black and brown artists than ever, and those like Giddens and Flemons now collaborate with major institutions and serve as cultural ambassadors. But as Giddens is the first to say, there's always more to do, more to learn, more to sing.*

—John Lingan

I. STORYTELLING ON A GRAND SCALE

THE BELIEVER: How does one learn that their opera has won a Pulitzer Prize?

RHIANNON GIDDENS: In this day and age, the answer shouldn't be surprising. I had put my son to bed and went for a walk, and Twitter beeped and I looked down and that was how I found out—from Twitter. I hadn't even remembered it was happening. You submit it [for consideration] but I hadn't even thought about it again after that. And then I turned around and there it was, a tweet! I sent it to my sister.

BLVR: You've written from enslaved people's points of view before, but why did this particular story, *Omar*, seem more like an opera than a song?

RG: Well, I was asked to write an opera. And I didn't really question whether this story should take that shape. Why not an opera? Like, why is this story not worthy of the opera treatment as much as *Othello* or *Aida*, any of these big, grand stories that have been set on the operatic stage? This is just as operatic as any of them. Opera, at its heart, is a cross-disciplinary collaboration that holds the biggest emotions that humans have. It's armies and deathless love and all the things we experience as humans. Opera is a container big enough to hold it all; it's a way to tell a story on a grand scale. And I don't know of a more dramatic story than that of a thirty-seven-year-old scholar stolen from his homeland and taken across the ocean in horrific circumstances to a place where he speaks none of the languages and manages to survive for over fifty years. That's operatic in scope to me.

Now, the issue is that our [contemporary] perspective on opera is very particular and narrow. When it started out, it was way more for everybody. Now it's seen as a high-class thing, and is completely absent from the culture. It's been taken over by movies and TV. [But] there is this renaissance that's happening right now in modern American opera that is not just coming from African American communities: *The Central Park Five*, *X: The Life and Times of Malcolm X*, even *Brokeback Mountain* and *Dead Man Walking*. Now you've got *Fire Shut Up in My Bones* by Terence Blanchard, and *Champion* by him as well. And these other pieces like *The Factotum*, which is Will Liverman's reimagining of *The Barber of Seville* in a Chicago barbershop, incorporating other aspects of Black music. There's a lot of innovation that's going on right now and new audiences coming to the opera house. And so it is exciting in that way, if it can be sustained. And I hope that *Omar* winning that prize keeps lifting the waters for everybody. Anytime we can actually challenge the status quo of who gets to be representative of the American story, I think we win.

BLVR: Tell me about your exposure to opera—and to folk music, for that matter. I understand that your father had a voice.

RG: Well, my dad was a singer, for sure. He still is. He went to the University of North Carolina Greensboro for music,

Photos by Ebru Yıldız.

and he was studying opera and classical music. He didn't end up staying, but he had a beautiful baritone, very much like how he was trained. So when he sang folk music, he sang it full-throated, just beautiful. Like my mom said, "He sang Schubert like it was butter." And I sang with him, and with my sister. My aunt is a singer. My cousin's a musician. My uncle was a bluegrass musician. The whole family is very musical. It was just kind of what we did. We'd sing folk revival songs. Not the roots stuff that I got into later, but you know: Peter, Paul and Mary, and Donovan. I wouldn't have heard opera outside of "What's Opera, Doc?" and those sorts of things.

When I was seventeen I went to a choral camp the summer of my senior year, and kind of fell in with musical-theater kids and people who were wanting to make music a career. I still couldn't read music really well, but I learned to fake-read, hold the paper, and sing with the other kids. I already knew how to sing harmonies, but [theater is] just great training, right? I got introduced to Sondheim. I didn't know any of this stuff.

So I decided to apply to music school. What I knew about opera, I got from watching one on TV. Might have been a Mozart [opera] or something; I don't remember. But I bought a couple of opera compilation CDs. They would have had, like, Domingo and Pavarotti and Montserrat Caballé and Mirella Freni and all these people sort of doing the hits. I applied to two schools, Carnegie Mellon and Oberlin. Carnegie Mellon's more of a musical-theater school, and Oberlin's more of an opera school. And I just knew that in opera, [you] didn't have to talk. That was the fear. In musical theater, you have to memorize dialogue and stuff, and I was just not into that. I still really didn't know what opera was. I had no idea what I was getting into; I just liked the idea of singing all the time. I chose to go to Oberlin. Then I learned what I had done to myself.

BLVR: What did you learn there that still informs the work you do now? What did that training do to your voice?

RG: I had to learn everything at once. I didn't know how to read music. I didn't know the Western art canon. I didn't know the repertoire. I didn't know everything. It was a really hard five years, and I loved every minute of it. But I was also in bits, crying at my teacher's studio, because I couldn't figure out how to learn this music, because I couldn't read music. There's something that's freeing about that, because I didn't know what the hell I was getting into. I sometimes think the less I know about something, the better, because then I just get in and ask, OK, how do I do this? How do I figure this out? Who can help me figure this out?

And that was opera. It's like a sport. It's athletic. There was somebody who said, "If you do a full opera and you're the main character, it's like a football game." Like, the same amount of calories spent. You're standing onstage and you're filling the entire hall with just your voice. I mean, it's remarkable, really. Everything after is kind of like, Well, it's not a three-hour opera that I just performed all in French with high Cs. I bring that same focus to a folk song or to whatever song we're doing. And I think it is unusual to shift that focus to the things I've done since. It's one of the things that makes me me.

II. SERVICE-BASED MUSIC

BLVR: So how did that transition start, from opera to folk?

RG: I graduated and came back to North Carolina and I didn't know how to use a microphone. I could play some guitar chords, but I'd never played the fiddle or banjo or anything. But when I came home, I started going to contra dances. They're like square dances, but in long lines. It's a European thing. There's this conversation between France and England going on with [the evolution of] this dance, and then it becomes English country dance. The things in the Jane Austen movies. But then in the States, it starts to change and gets combined with other things. And then a lot of times, the players for these dancers are African American because the dance musician is a servant position. Enslaved people become the dance bands. And then you have things like quadrilles and these sorts of square formations starting to turn into square dances in places like Kentucky and North Carolina. This is all scholarship that Phil Jamison has published.

When I started, I was mostly dancing with older white people; I was usually the only [Black] one, the raisin in the oatmeal. But I loved the live-music aspect of it. I started hearing this banjo music that I'd never heard. This old-time plunky thing. I'd only heard bluegrass and I was like, What is that sound? That's amazing. And I met the band Gaelwynd at a contra dance. They played Scottish and Irish tunes and were doctors by day or whatever. I was this twenty-three-year-old fresh out of opera school and they were looking for a singer. Those poor folks; I learned how to sing on a microphone doing gigs with them and learned how to start changing my diction singing these Irish songs. And this is before I had done my research and I'm just making the bouzouki player wince with my overdone diction and vibrato. They're all lovely; I'm still friends with all of them. I listened to a butt-ton of music that was being put out under the "Celtic" moniker, wondering how I could find a way to that kind of singing but still be me and not fake. [*Singing operatically*] "I wish I was on yonder hill." I mean, I could do that, but it's not me.

So it's all kind of happening at the same time. And then there's the moment when I'm like, I want to get the fiddle and the banjo and I want to start learning during all this. I'm an administrative assistant during the day and then have this other life. I took a second job at the Macaroni Grill as a singing hostess to buy my fiddle and banjo. I started learning fiddle from Nora Garver in the Celtic band. I would play twin

---

MICROINTERVIEW WITH VICTOR OLADIPO, PART III

THE BELIEVER: You're a professional hooper, so you probably don't have a bunch of free time for creative exploration. Who has been a major support in helping you develop your skills and passion as a professional singer? Did you train formally at any point?

VICTOR OLADIPO: I've had the opportunity to work with a lot of people who are respected in music. But I've never taken a music or vocal lesson. I'd love to start. That could be the next step for me. Learning how to control my voice better. I think I could really take my talent to a new place when I find time [to take a vocal class]. I've never taken any lessons, though. It's just what I feel. I just sing what I feel. And I've collaborated with vocalists, songwriters, musicians. ✶

fiddle with her. But then I met Joe Thompson, the African American fiddler. He was eighty-six years old. That's kind of where my final education started, really.

BLVR: You and your bandmates in the Carolina Chocolate Drops had a kind of apprenticeship under him, right?

RG: That's the next five years of training. When I found Joe, it was like, Oh god, he's from the town my family's from. We're related up in the family tree. I know this man. I recognize—I could see myself in this music. That was a really important piece of it too. I feel very lucky because there's nothing better for an opera singer than to be the banjo player in a dance band. Because that's what the Chocolate Drops were at the beginning. We were a dance and old-time band, and then we had other things we could play. I started as a caller. I would call dances. Service-based music, that's what that is, because you're there to serve the dancers: if the dancers weren't there, you wouldn't be there. And I often say the best way to start out is with dancers and kids because they're two of the most honest audiences you'll ever have. If you're hitting it, you see it in the dancers' bodies.

Being a caller is being responsible for people. You're in charge of the whole evening. How do you keep it flowing? How do you teach the dance? I did that for years: I would go around and call different dances, then started playing for the dances, and then started playing with Joe. The foundation, I think, of what follows for me is this combination of the exacting classical approach and the service and community orientation that came next. This idea of telling the history of this music, of supporting an eighty-seven-, eighty-eight-year-old man as he got older—I think all that is just an antidote to the bullshit that goes on in the music industry. Starting with that focus has kept me on a path, I think, that feels real.

III. "TELLING OTHER PEOPLE'S STORIES"

BLVR: How did you develop such an interest in telling other people's stories? That's been a constant in your songwriting and now your opera as well.

RG: Well, it came from the very fact that we don't know what we think we know, and what we're being told is—they're not even trying to hide the fact that it's just lies. You kind of go, OK, this thing I was told my entire life, that the banjo was invented by white people in Appalachia—it's not just a little bit wrong. It's not like it was invented by white people in Arkansas or Maine, or by Irish people, which I've been told before. It was invented by enslaved Africans in the Caribbean! I mean, if that is so wrong, what else have I been told that is *that* wrong? It's like, if that is so wrong, what else don't I know?

And then the corollary is always: In whose best interest is it that I don't know these things? In whose best interest is it that these divisive narratives have become truth for people? Because it's always in somebody's best interest. Nobody makes this shit up just for the fun of it. It's got to be working on lots of different levels. You've got to have a grand plan of white supremacy. And it's not a conspiracy; it's not like there's some mastermind behind it. It's just the way of American thought. England practiced genocide on Irish and Scottish people by saying that Gaels, who have one of the oldest literate languages in Europe, were savages. They wanted land, so they used this rhetoric of race. Then you have trans-Saharan Arabic slave traders talking about sub-Saharan Blacks being natural slaves.

These racial attitudes that have already existed for a while come together in this unholy alliance during the economic

---

MICROINTERVIEW WITH VICTOR OLADIPO, PART IV

THE BELIEVER: What other vocalists have you been inspired by?

VICTOR OLADIPO: Jamie Foxx. Maybe surprisingly. Some might not consider him a musician, but I look at him as a role model because of his versatility. He's someone I've admired for a while, and I met him at [the NBA] All-Star Weekend in LA [in 2018]. I was walking out, he was walking in. We stopped and talked and I actually sang one of my songs to him and he started to sing it with me. That was amazing. Vocally, I've also been influenced by Usher, Chris Brown. It's hard to pick just one. That's tough. Also, people automatically think that, as a male, I only listen to male R&B, but I gotta show my females love, too, dawg. H.E.R., Jazmine Sullivan, Whitney. Tremendous influences and I'm grateful for their music. From the Queen, Beyoncé, to whoever is [just starting out], I'm listening to it. ★

Photos by Rosie Cohe.

explosion that happens around the slave trade. I mean, people are making money hand over fist. So it is in everybody's best interest to reinforce this racial notion of a permanent underclass. When you're looking at where white supremacy comes from, I mean, it's just literally enforcement of the status quo to maintain the wealth of the many in the hands of the few. That's it. And it's an underclass of all colors, where everybody has one thing in common. They're all poor. That's why this narrative is so fucking important, because it strikes at the heart of anywhere those people come together. Poor white people, poor brown people, poor Black people, living together.

BLVR: What role does music play in all this? And how is your own music a response to it?

RG: We're so often told, *Well, you guys do this kind of music, and you guys do this kind of music, and you don't really do each other's music.* But take the banjo, which used to be an instrument that everybody played. There were Black people playing [banjos] in the Caribbean as ceremonial instruments,

as sort of spiritual instruments. It becomes a dance band instrument in North America. And by the 1820s and '30s, it's starting to transfer over to European American hands and people in rural areas.

There were Black people in Appalachia; there were brown people in Appalachia. There was all this mixing going on constantly, continuously, everywhere. Thousands of interactions, millions of interactions. And so the banjo is starting to be played by everybody. The first recorded instance of banjo and fiddle being played together is by Black people playing them in Rhode Island in [1756]. It's a pan-American instrument. There are banjo orchestras. There's a famous Black banjo player who's a celebrity in Australia.

But this all starts to change by the early twentieth century. Because you still have blackface minstrelsy, though it's starting to go underground in the nineteen-teens. You have [*The*] *Birth of a Nation* and the rejuvenated Ku Klux Klan and this growing idea that there's too many immigrants. You see the rhetoric happening, this obsession with mongrelization. Henry Ford is very vocal about the "jungle

music" of the time, and he's very anti-Semitic, so he sees an unholy coalition between Blacks and Jews. And that's when you really start seeing this idea of the banjo and Appalachia being an ethnically pure receptacle for good old-fashioned Anglo culture.

BLVR: You live in Ireland, whose influence is foundational to US music and culture, especially in the Appalachian region you're describing. What are you learning from it? Are you playing or learning more Irish music?

RG: Irish music is foundational and a major pillar of the creation of the unique American sound. I, however, think it's more foundational in the Atlantic world, from the Caribbean up to the centers in New York, the waterways, Baltimore. That's where Irish music, I think, really inserts itself. But I don't think it's more than German tunes or English tunes or Welsh tunes or Scottish tunes [in Appalachia].

The recording of Irish music in America during the 1920s is what revitalized the Irish traditional movement. Not a lot of people know that. But it was dying out in Ireland because the culture was being murdered by the English. A lot of that culture was tied to Gaelic speakers, and the aristocracy had fled hundreds of years before. So there was not any kind of reinvestment in the native Gaelic culture. It was being pushed out along with the people because of the famine. And then by the '20s, Ireland was fighting for its independence, and impoverished. They didn't really value that music in that culture. It was being kind of invaded by English culture.

This is not answering your question, but that is what drives me; because that's more interesting and it's more true than these nationalistic narratives that were told.

IV. "WHAT IS ART FOR, REALLY?"

BLVR: That same drive—to dissolve boundaries and false narratives—must inform your work with the Silkroad Ensemble. What's your relationship with Yo-Yo Ma?

RG: My first memory of Yo-Yo would be because I had one of his records, *Haydn: Cello Concertos*. It was one of the handful of classical music CDs I had when I went to college, and I had it memorized. From then on, I knew him as a famous classical guy who I never would have anticipated meeting.

And then Silkroad reached out and asked me if I would join them for a song on their *Sing Me Home* record. It was a record full of different vocalists. I did a recording session with them and met Yo-Yo for the first time, and it was a great experience. He's a talker; he loves to talk about philosophy and life. We sat and asked each other: What can we do with this art to make the world a better place?

He was already really thinking about what music meant for him. This was some years ago. He told me his story: He's been playing cello since he was able to hold an instrument. And he's been famous for almost that long. I mean, he's playing for President Kennedy when he's seven or whatever. It's crazy. And he said he realized as he became an adult that he played cello because that's what he'd always done. And he realized he was getting to the point where that wasn't enough, to be doing something just because that's what you knew how to do. A lot of classical musicians find themselves in that place.

He was at the point where he realized, I actually have to choose playing the cello every day. I should never do it as a default. And I was really struck by that because I thought, Here's this guy who can do whatever he wants and he's thinking in these terms. It was a good conversation for me because I'm never going to be as famous as Yo-Yo Ma, but I feel like we're in a similar sphere. We've done a lot of things and we're really trying to answer that question: What is art for, really?

For me, the cultural ambassadorship is hand in glove with the story of the banjo, and I've always felt that mission.

I mean, I was just at the airport and this Black TSA agent was like, "Here, give me your guitar up here," and I was like, "Well, it's a banjo," and he's like, "All I can think of is *Deliverance*." If I had a dime... But, you know, every moment like that is an opportunity. I'm going to go through the whole *You know who invented the banjo, right?* Blah, blah, blah, blah. And that's one more Black person who knows that. My daughter was just patting me on the shoulder in the airport.

MICROINTERVIEW WITH VICTOR OLADIPO, PART V

THE BELIEVER: At what point did you realize music could be something to pursue more seriously? I read about how you were encouraged early on by Quinn Cook, who you grew up with. But beyond those fun times with friends and teammates, when did you have that "I want to do this" moment?

VICTOR OLADIPO: It's funny because Quinn was one of the first people outside my family to know I could sing—as a teammate, as a friend. I used to go to his house in sixth grade. We spent countless hours in his room looking up music videos on his computer, making beats. We have "Go-Go" music down here [in Washington, DC], and I would sing and he'd play the audio. He has bragging rights to initiating my singing career. [*Laughs*] He's a brother, family. It runs way deeper than friendship. He made me comfortable enough to sing around my other teammates. Eventually it trickled down and people found out in college, and I performed at my university. In 2013, my first year in the league, players weren't really sharing their gifts like that. The norm wasn't really about sharing all your other passions. It was just playing basketball. That's what you did: you were a basketball player. I sort of second-guessed myself. Basketball swag is high, aggressive—it's sports. Would people relate to me and be cool if I wasn't rapping? Rapping is hard—it's taken seriously. But singing is seen as soft. After I released my first album, *Songs for You*, [in 2017] and then won the Most Improved Player Award [in 2018], I realized I could kill you with both. It was like, OK, you just got bodied by the singing guy. Early on I used to question myself: Will people take me seriously? But you just gotta do it 'cause you love it. I learned that as I got older. Just keep sharing your message. ★

She's like, "I know, Mom." But I can't help myself, because I'm just like, This is kind of why I'm here. And I don't know what that'll do in that man's life. He may immediately forget it or he may not. I've seen people be really struck by it.

BLVR: How does the Silkroad Ensemble allow you to further that mission, the "cultural ambassadorship"?

RG: It decenters me. And my tradition, which I think is important because I've been focused on it for so long. You know, the United States and African American tradition and the banjo—I've been focused on that for so long, and you get into Silkroad, all of a sudden I'm in a larger global context. That's the way forward for me. I'm very steeped in the history of the United States and have mined that for a lot of artistic ways to connect people to history, but ultimately, it has to be connected to a larger story of human migration, of global movements and global collaboration.

Silkroad was also an opportunity to continue making my point that diversity in America isn't new. It's *so* not new. It's beyond not new. It's even beyond thinking people are Black, white, or red. There's every shade of brown in between. And I think it's important to remind people in America that we're not unique, and how many things that we call American have roots all over the world. You know, I think that's why American music is so popular: everybody sees a piece of themselves in it. It's important to say we're just a link in a chain.

V. "ONCE BEYONCÉ PICKS UP THE BANJO, MY JOB IS DONE"

BLVR: Your new solo album has very little of that old American banjo tradition, and its influences are certainly diverse. Have you felt edged out of that country-music mold because of the narrow expectations for success?

RG: There was a time when I could have gone down that road. I could be a pop-country singer right now. I've got the voice. I had the looks and the size and all that shit at one point. I could have made a go at it. When T-Bone Burnett had me do a solo record [in 2015], if I'd had a bucketful of original songs and a desire to be a country singer, that would have been the moment. But that's not who I am. I kind of walked in the other direction. I might not have been successful if I

had tried to do that, but I did my own thing and on my own terms, and I am proud of that.

But I am dying for some big, famous person—in the Black community, specifically—to pay attention. I've said it in interviews: I won a fucking Pulitzer for an opera about an African that was enslaved. A Muslim. It's our history, you know? But, like, nobody cares in that world. Not one interview from any mainstream Black press. On top of the Grammys, on top of the MacArthur, they just don't care. I don't know if I'm not dark enough or I'm not Black enough or whatever. Would I like more Black people at my concerts? Sure. Would I like some interest from the mainstream Black media? Sure, but I know I'm niche. So OK, fine. Can somebody over there pick up the damn banjo? Once Beyoncé picks up the banjo, my job is done.

I don't want it to be a punch line or anything. I just want it to be available and for more people to know they have a right, they have stock in that. There are now so many people of color playing the banjo and playing that music and writing their music. It's available out there if people get hip to it, but the resistance is so strong.

BLVR: But it certainly seems like there's been increased attention to diversity in the country/Americana world, at least among certain artists, writers, and audiences.

RG: You have not seen an equivalent movement of Black people into the audience. I mean, it's happening slowly. And I will say that I've talked to good numbers of independent and non-mainstream Black journalists. But there is a huge disconnect I feel between mainstream Black culture and what's happening in the Americana and bluegrass spaces, these acoustic spaces. There are more young Black people there. The numbers are still small, but it is happening. And it will be happening more beyond me because I'm just too old, or old-fashioned. Even the new record is full of old-fashioned songs.

I chose to leave Nashville. I was just tired of being the token. And it's not that I was the only one, but I felt like I was being trotted out anytime Americana wanted this and that. I'm good friends with those folks; we've talked about it. And I recognized that I was, you know, serving a purpose, and so I would go do these things. But I felt very alone.

Now there's a concentration of similar-minded people within Nashville. It feels weird sometimes, because I won't say I've been forgotten, but, like, I do feel like that movement has kind of moved on without me. It's kind of, you know, continued on. But someone like Brandi Carlile, she can do things that I simply cannot do; she's far bigger, a kingmaker. So I'm like, All right, they got that covered now. I will go elsewhere. I had already kind of started moving, like doing the Silkroad and writing the opera. I go where the universe is telling me to go. Where are my talents best used?

It's the reason I left opera in the first place. Then the new opera opportunity came to me, the ballet came to me, and they were so uniquely suited to what I do. How could I imagine this? I don't—I can't imagine the next step. I couldn't have imagined writing kids' books. I couldn't have imagined any of the stuff that's happened. So I'm in the phase of, like, really kind of taking stock, asking, What am I supposed to do?

BLVR: It sounds like you're having your Yo-Yo Ma moment.

RG: You have existential crises in this industry all the time, because there's always fear of missing out. There's always, What is so-and-so doing? Oh, they got a billboard. I didn't get a billboard. They sold out and I didn't sell out. It's just constant. All this shit that it's like, I don't have any control over that. All I can do is use the tools I've been given.

I'm in a real philosophical space. I'm forty-six years old, and why am I here? I mean, that never stops, right? You think you know and then it changes. I'm very proud of the work I've done, and now I'm kind of going, What is it that I'm supposed to continue to do? Am I supposed to keep flying

---

SONGS WITH *ZOMBIE* IN THE TITLE (THAT AREN'T ABOUT LITERAL ZOMBIES)

✶ "Zombie" by the Cranberries
✶ "Zombie Girl" by Adrianne Lenker
✶ "Zombie" by Jamie T
✶ "They Are Night Zombies!! They are Neighbors!! They Have Come Back From the Dead!! Ahhhh!" by Sufjan Stevens
✶ "Zombie" by Fela Kuti
✶ "Astro Zombies" by the Misfits

—list compiled by Claire Fairtlough

---

around this fucking planet, playing for a thousand people here, five hundred here, two thousand here, eight hundred here, eating up gas? Am I supposed to keep doing that? I don't know. I loved acting in the TV show *Nashville*. But do I start doing auditions?

I've been very close to being on Broadway. Twice. The first time I was actually in New York, about to replace Audra McDonald in *Shuffle Along*, and they shut down the show. When something like that happens, you either go, I'm going to double down and I'm going to move to New York and I'm going to be on Broadway. Or you go, OK, well, that wasn't meant to be. The other Broadway thing, John Turturro was like, *I've got this script and I just think you'd be perfect for it.* And we worked on it during the pandemic. He gave me acting lessons through Zoom. I had a coach I was working with on all this shit. I, like, actually sat and read a scene with De Niro. And then they couldn't get the funding and blah, blah, blah.

It's just all these weird-ass near misses for the kinds of things that could possibly catapult somebody into another level of stardom. Those things continuously fail for me. So it's like, what do you do with that? You go, I was meant to do something else with my time. And then the opera does so great. I really do believe in that—you know, movements and energies and all that. You can find the thing you were best suited for. It's a struggle.

VI. GOOD OLD-FASHIONED FUN

BLVR: Especially in light of that, how did *You're the One* emerge? It's all original songs, a milestone for you. Was that something the universe presented?

RG: To misquote Jane Austen, it's a truth universally acknowledged that original material gets more attention, more opportunities to reach more people. I've never been like one of those songwriters where I just broke up with my boyfriend and I'm going to write an album's worth of material. I don't like writing about myself, per se. I just think other people do that and they have lives that are interesting enough to do that. I don't. But I've enjoyed learning to be a songwriter and I'm collaborating on songs. And I am not prolific, but I have had a steady kind of trickle of songs I've written that I didn't put on any project, because I'm so focused on the history and the stories I'm trying to tell.

I got to a point where it's like, Let's go back to having a full band onstage. Ultimately, it's a fun record. I haven't done that. I try and walk that tightrope to make people feel like they should take responsibility for their education, but not make them feel like I'm castigating them for something they have no control over, in terms of the history of the United States. You have to be an artist who makes people have fun too. I needed a palate cleanser. I needed a break and to explore other aspects of my art and my music and my voice. I have to keep learning. I'm an obsessive learner.

BLVR: How did that attitude affect the writing and recording—the sound, in other words?

RG: We had a big studio in Miami, Criteria, that's seen a lot of famous records. The core of Jack Splash's guys are all young Black men who play at church together. They're mega, mega talented. And then I brought my guys I've been playing with over the years, a bunch of acoustic instruments, accordions, banjos, fiddles, stand-up bass, acoustic guitar. And we found this path through the sounds, and that's what I'm most excited about. I mean, my own songwriting

---

MICROINTERVIEW WITH VICTOR OLADIPO, PART VI

THE BELIEVER: As a musician, who's your favorite NBA counterpart? All-time, there's dudes like Shaq, Rony Seikaly, Allen Iverson. And right now there's Damian Lillard, Aaron Gordon, Iman Shumpert.

VICTOR OLADIPO: I love Damian Lillard's music. He's reaching the world on a much larger spectrum. He's been so successful with both rapping and basketball. He's really good. But there's a few others I listen to as well: Marvin Bagley, Lonzo Ball. There's lots of guys who have entered this space with talent. JaVale McGee produces. Lou Williams raps. There's such a plethora. Shaq. A lot of us really love music and sports. Not just in the NBA either. There are upcoming artists who are athletes. like Flau'jae [Johnson of Louisiana State University]. We're just showcasing our talents more than ever. ✶

is whatever. I think there's some good tunes in there, but I think the sound we created is really hip. It sounds like nothing else. We made it in, like, six days. You just go, *Here's the song and let's cut it.*

But this is not, you know, "Rhiannon Goes Pop." I had a bunch of songs and I found a good partner in Jack Splash. And I said to him very clearly, "I want to use sound worlds that I haven't used, and that's what you represent. But I also want to be myself. I don't want my fan base to be like, *Oh god, she fucking sold out.*" I could have gone to some really hip pop producer and said, *Here's some songs. Make them into pop songs.* But I didn't want to do that. [Jack] and I found this middle place. He thought the budget wasn't going to allow live tracking with everybody and I was like, "I will forego whatever I would make to have us all in the same place at the same time." A few of those songs were, like, ten and eleven people tracking at once. Super old-fashioned.

BLVR: Speaking of old-fashioned, one of my favorite songs on the album is "Who Are You Dreaming Of." It has this lovely mid-century, orchestral feel, unlike anything I've heard you do. How was it to sing like that?

RG: In another time, I would have been an interpreter in a gown with a big hanging microphone. That's what my voice is, you know? There is a world where I would love to go out with an orchestra just doing those songs or the old PBS special, singing the American songbook or whatever. But "Who Are You Dreaming Of" was a way to slip into that world.

Francesco [Turrisi, Giddens's partner and musical collaborator] and I just did a vocal and piano recital. I had a microphone, obviously, but I just sang for an hour and a half, in about five or six different languages, because we were kind of messing around with that whole idea of a classical recital, where you always do different languages. But we had, like, '70s Italian pop songs, next to a classical piece, next to a bolero from Cuba.

It all belongs together, and that's what people used to do. And there is a dream that when I'm older, I can ascend to my elder-statesman-hood by doing those sorts of performances. I would love to do that in the future. Do an Ethel Waters, Bessie Smith, and Alberta Hunter tribute show or something. There's so many... I mean, there's never a dearth of ideas, that's for sure. I would be dead before I'm bored. ✶

THE DESERT

AND THE

RIVER

IN THE FACE OF A JIHADIST
MOVEMENT THAT SEEKS TO
SUPPRESS ALL CREATIVE
EXPRESSION, MALIAN FOLK STAR
VIEUX FARKA TOURÉ IS ATTEMPTING
TO PRESERVE HIS COUNTRY'S MOST
PRIZED MUSICAL TRADITIONS.

by

ROB
CURRAN

Illustration by CLAIRE MERCHLINSKY
Photography by ANNIE RISEMBERG

1.

hen I arrive at Vieux Farka Touré's house, he is rehearsing with his band in a colonnaded courtyard. It's a kind of residential amphitheater, about thirty yards square, with nothing in it but a couple of mango trees, a handful of vehicles, and the band. The musicians and extended family who live with Vieux are milling around in the sunshine, giving the place the feel of a tropical Graceland or the South of France villa where the Stones recorded

Exile on Main St. Vieux does not miss a beat as he gestures for me to sit next to him, nor does he miss a beat when he's signaling to his uniformed security guard to answer the phone or to brew a round of green tea.

Vieux's face drifts from his trademark boyish smile to pursed concentration as he exchanges looks with his new band member, a player of the mandolin-like n'goni, who is sitting on the other side of him. Picking the strings horizontally with his right index finger as if coaxing the sounds out of them, Vieux begins to play the traditional "Diarabi," a cri de coeur from a young man to his lover's disapproving parents.

The other band members join in and music fills the courtyard. It's at once raw and polished, a refined jamming, Vieux's special blend of traditional Malian and American roots music known as the desert blues. Some tunes pulsate with such raucous joy that the statue of Vieux Farka Touré's father, Ali—the man who made "Diarabi" famous—could be forgiven for tapping a golden foot from his perch at a traffic circle at the end of the street.

"Where I am from," Vieux says, "there's the desert and there's the river, and everything we do has the desert and the river in it."

When Vieux starts to sing, it's easy to imagine the river. On the surface, his voice is deep and laconic, but there's an undercurrent of sadness, an ancient ululation. Here in Bamako, Mali, the Niger River is the central feature, like the Mississippi River in Memphis, if the Mississippi were still clean enough to have vibrant grassy shores and children swimming off its docks.

Then, in the middle of the song, Vieux stops and gives a subtle signal. Everything stops. Vieux makes his band tick with the precision of his smart watch. He's a bandleader in the maximal, demanding style of Prince or of James Brown—the two-hundred-gigs-a-year, holler-till-your-last-vocal-cord-expires kind of bandleader. He doesn't let his band or himself off the hook.

"He pushes me," his backing singer, Muhamed Dicko, told me later. "I need someone to push me. I have his support. When he's in Bamako he asks me to play with him. Gives me visibility."

where the Sahara dunes meet the Sahel scrubland, are the hubs of this music.

Currently, the ancient city is under a blockade by jihadist groups, who have plagued the region for more than a decade. Right now, nothing comes into or out of Timbuktu, nothing but the Niger River, and those lucky enough to escape. Some of those people, like Dicko, are bound to end up at Vieux's house, living or recording there or both. The French army, which has kept the jihadists at bay since 2012, recently pulled out of Mali. The United Nations peacekeeping forces are pulling out. Even international aid organizations are likely to scale down operations. But Vieux Farka Touré will not be moved.

"A musician with his stature could live anywhere he wanted to, but he chooses to stay, in a less comfortable situation than he'd have elsewhere, and he chooses to do it for Mali," said Andy Jordan, the Denton, Texas, musician who introduced me to Vieux's music.

Vieux tours about half the year, but he always comes back to Bamako. He is currently recording an album for Dicko's band in his home studio. When Dicko can't get gigs around Bamako, Vieux sends money home to the man's family. There are rules, though—rules that echo the discipline once required to work with Prince.

"I don't drink or smoke. Nobody in my band drinks or smokes. I have to have them all clean," said Vieux.

In the courtyard that day, Dicko gets no charity. Vieux gives him some stern notes on the performance of the high-tempo "Adou."

"You don't sing with your mouth," Vieux tells Dicko, pulling at his own

But Vieux is also dealing with concerns that stretch far behind those of a standard bandleader. When the jihadists came to his native region of Timbuktu, and threatened the lives of many relatives and musicians—in Dicko's case, literally—Vieux opened his home, and his home studio, to them.

Malian traditional music is a vital element of world heritage. It's a direct conduit to a forgotten classical school of learning that rivals those of Alexandria, Egypt, and Athens, Greece. Many musicologists believe Malian traditional music is the source water of the Delta blues, which is one reason Ali and Vieux Farka Touré and their peers have mixed the two so seamlessly into the desert blues. Timbuktu and the semidesert north of the country, cheeks to demonstrate. "You sing from your gut."

Later, Vieux tells me: "They think they have to be like Michael Jackson. I say, 'Just be yourself. It's your voice. Don't try to do what other people are doing.'"

I was first brought to Vieux's house by Phil Paoletta, the imperturbable American hotelier, West African music aficionado, blogger, Bamako TikTok star, lapsed sheep farmer, Timbuktu calligraphy preservationist, and motorbike tour guide. Phil was first brought to Vieux's house by a man wearing animal skins, who carried a sword everywhere "for security reasons." It was their tendency to say yes to things that Phil and Vieux bonded over (that, and the fact that Phil's wife is part of the Dogon ethnic group, whose members have traditionally been "joking cousins" with Vieux's Songhai people, making it obligatory for them to tease one another).

Vieux can never say no to a guest, or to having a guest star on his records. Part of this may be strategic: collaboration made his father, Ali, world-famous, giving him three Grammy-winning albums. Mostly, however, Vieux just loves having people around, and above all, people with whom he can jam.

When Vieux met the Israeli experimental pianist Idan Raichel at a German airport, it was inevitable they would end up collaborating. They performed at a show in Tel Aviv together, and were persuaded by Raichel's manager to continue the jam session in the studio. The result was one of the most intriguing Jewish-Muslim artistic collaborations of the modern era. The Touré-Raichel Collective produced two ambient masterpieces—elegant, unforced, soothing pieces of work.

Vieux's ultimate collaborator, of course, remains his late father. In all Vieux's musical projects, he pays homage to his legacy. Vieux could easily be slowed down by the weight of his pedigree. Not even Hamlet had to circle a golden statue of his father every time he drove home. Ali Farka Touré is a giant of Malian culture. Paul Chandler, an American who has dedicated his life to the preservation of traditional Malian music, realized the unique power Ali possessed when he promoted events in parts of the country that were heavily affected by jihadist violence.

"While we were traveling, even in 2014, 2015, when things were still a little raw between communities and it was hard to get everyone to come together for an event, the one thing we noticed was if we did a night in honor of Ali Farka Touré, no matter what, people would always come together around him," said Chandler.

Most artists would find such legacies oppressive. Yet Vieux and Ali are perhaps the most successful musical dynasty since the Strauss family dominated the Viennese 1-2-3s for a century. After Ali's death, in 2006, Vieux chose to jam with the man's ghost rather than wrestle with it. Vieux plays a brand of Ali Farka Touré's desert blues, but he has pushed further into the mesmeric side of the music, working with reverb and a series of collaborators to get funky. In doing so, Vieux has reinvented his father's work as a kind of space rock. The boldest experiment in this vein was *Ali*, the 2022 album with Houston indie band Khruangbin.

"This is a thing I wanted to do for a long time, to play Ali's music at another level, to bring Ali's music to young people," said Vieux.

Keeping Ali's music alive is a challenge now that northern Mali is entering the second decade of a cultural and religious war that's set to worsen with the departure of UN forces. The jihadists would like nothing more than to destroy the musical and artistic traditions Ali represents. Nevertheless, Vieux continues tending the flame, touring and supporting Malian musicians. He just makes sure his bodyguard is never far away.

2.

Vieux Farka Touré was born in 1981 in Niafunké, a riverside town about a hundred miles south along the Niger River from Timbuktu, the cultural center of Mali, and five hundred miles northeast of Bamako, the capital and largest city. During Vieux's childhood, Niafunké would become synonymous with his father, becoming a kind of African version of Willie Nelson's musical fiefdom in Austin, Texas. Vieux grew up in a time of promise for Mali and West Africa, in contrast to the West Africa that his father was born into. Ali was the only surviving son of ten that his mother bore. In recognition of this perseverance, Ali was given the nickname "Farka," the Songhai word for "donkey." In Mali, donkeys still carry some of the heaviest burdens.

Ali's rise to fame was not instantaneous. He competed in national singing contests and composed songs in several different languages, steadily building a reputation around Mali.

would sing an old song dedicated to another "Samba." Vieux remembers dancing while Grand-père sang.

In his spare time, Vieux listened to American radio and cassettes, geeking out on Jimi Hendrix—with whom he has been compared—John Lee Hooker, B.B. King, and Phil Collins, among other artists. He taught himself the guitar, playing along to cassettes of his father. Vieux was not the only great Malian musician to learn this way. Ibrahim Ag Alhabib, a founding member of the legendary Tuareg band Tinariwen, learned to play with a guitar he made out of an oil can and a bicycle brake line, strumming along to Ali Farka Touré's music, according to the band's website.

In 1992, Ali met American slide guitarist Ry Cooder while both were gigging around London, and they discovered they were mutual fans. In the space of five years, Cooder would feature on three of the great fusion records of all time, working with Indian slide guitarist V. M. Bhatt, with Cuba's Buena Vista Social Club, and with Ali on *Talking Timbuktu*. That 1994 album won Ali the first of three Grammy Awards, global recognition, and in turn made him a local and national hero.

Vieux had started to learn the calabash—a hemisphere hewn from a gourd and played with slight drumsticks—so he could accompany his father. When it came time for Vieux to graduate from secondary school, his father confronted him. Ali did not want Vieux to become a musician.

If Vieux was hurt by his father's refusal to take him into the family business, those feelings are now gone. He looks back on that talk as the kind of

Vieux was Ali's second son, a special status in the Tourés' Songhai culture, which earned him the name "Samba" in the Songhai language.

Vieux sought collaboration with his father from babyhood. He often sat in on his father's practice sessions, internalizing the mixture of traditional and rock music that Ali was inventing. After he was sent to bed, Vieux would sneak back to the rehearsal room, his

mother said. He was witnessing the development of Ali into someone who would become universally renowned as one of the greatest electric guitarists ever.

With his father often on tour, Vieux spent a lot of time with Ali's brother in Nioro, a town closer to Bamako. His uncle was a driver for a cattle company. Another relative, a grand-uncle whom Vieux called his grandfather, goals-oriented career advice so many young graduates receive from their parents.

The reason Ali discouraged his son was "because there are so many problems with musicians. People were coming from Europe to take the music," said Vieux. "They told them: *We're going to produce a record.* They kept the music, and they kept all the money."

In the book *Mali Blues: Traveling to an African Beat*, about another giant of the local scene, Boubacar "Kar Kar" Traoré, author Lieve Joris captures how alien the music industry felt to the traditional men of the Sahel. Kar Kar told the author that he was flown to the United States by a promoter during his first effort to break into the Western charts. Years later, he ran into the man in Paris and the man ignored him. Kar Kar was flabbergasted that this American businessman, who had acted like his best friend the last time they met, could walk past him without so much as a greeting.

Ali felt just as ambivalent about his musical career, sometimes even introducing himself as a farmer or a mechanic, according to legend. At one time, he felt his soul was wounded by his spiritual journeys on the guitar. In another unexpected move for a folk superstar, Ali would become mayor of Niafunké. He had celebrated the dusty old town so lovingly in his songs that the community couldn't help but love him back.

Ali recommended that his son enter the army. With that kind of career, his salary would be steady, work plentiful, and advancement likely. In the Songhai culture, it's important to carry on the work of your forefathers, and Vieux's

grandfather—after whom he was named—had been a soldier. Ali sent Vieux to stay with his dear friend Captain Ousmane Maiga, who would help Vieux prepare for life as an army officer. A year later, Vieux went to Maiga and said he was not taking to the military life. He wanted to play music.

Finally, his father relented. Instead of entering the army, Vieux Farka Touré was admitted to the Institut National des Arts in Bamako, where he mastered the calabash and began experimenting with guitar. Rather than directly guiding his son's artistic education, Ali arranged for Vieux to play with his friend Toumani Diabaté, a man whose family has reputedly worked as griots for seventy generations, and who is renowned as the greatest living player of the kora harp, an elaborate twenty-one-stringed instrument. Musicians in

West Africa are usually born into the trade, coming from clans dubbed griots by the French and known as jelis in Malian languages. Like the wandering Celtic harpists known as bards, griots were songsmiths for hire. Like bards, they often attached themselves to royal families and composed songs of praise for them. Today, they retain ceremonial roles at weddings, baptisms, and other events. They also keep the secrets of the production and playing of instruments like the n'goni, the marimba-like balafon, and the kora.

Vieux began playing the calabash with his father's band. In 2004, his father brought him to a festival in Privas, France. His dad asked him to warm up the crowd of ten thousand by playing a few solo tunes on a guitar that Ali had gifted to him. Vieux remembers the immense pressure ahead of that performance.

But he was hooked. By this time, he had developed a distinctive guitar technique, which some critics say draws on the conventions of the kora. It is characterized by rapid, polyrhythmic plucking with the thumb and index finger. He began working on his debut album. In the midst of recording, however, Ali was diagnosed with bone cancer. Before his father died, Vieux took Ali on a vacation to the banks of Lake Débo. There, Ali taught him the song "Tabara." Back in Bamako, weak from the cancer, Ali insisted on going into the studio to play with Vieux on "Tabara" and on two other songs for his son's debut. They were the last recordings Ali ever made. Vieux soon returned the favor, working on his father's last musical project, singing and drumming on the Grammy-winning, posthumous

album *Ali and Toumani*. Later, Vieux would produce an album of unreleased Ali tunes, *Voyageur*.

In the aughts, there was a swell of interest in Malian music. Capitalizing on this, Mohamed Aly "Manny" Ansar, a promoter of Tinariwen, started the Festival au Désert, initially held in the band's home region of Kidal. Later, the festival moved closer to the more accessible city of Timbuktu. Robert Plant, the lead singer of Led Zeppelin, came to play the festival. Blur singer Damon Albarn raved about it in the British music press. Bono attended as a guest. The festival also drew hundreds of young music fans from the West. The Westerners mixed with local Tuareg people. Vieux was one of the headliners, alongside other Malian stars, including female artist Oumou Sangaré, whose traditional-sounding songs often have a feminist twist.

After his Festival au Désert performances, Vieux's profile continued to grow. He played alongside the Dave Matthews Band—another of his myriad collaborators—as well as Shakira, Tinariwen, and others at the opening ceremony of the 2010 FIFA World Cup in South Africa. He had officially risen to international prominence. His second album, *Fondo*, reached number five on the Billboard World Album charts. He was making more money than he ever had. But back home, there was a crisis brewing.

Timbuktu was quickly becoming a stronghold for an offshoot of al-Qaeda. The semiarid Sahel lands were out of the reach of local military and law enforcement. Jihadists moved in and took advantage of this to launch attacks and kidnapping raids in Mali

and Algeria, then disappear to hideouts. The Festival au Désert had continued despite this. But in 2011, the jihadists snatched three young tourists from the center of Timbuktu and killed a fourth. Few overseas visitors came for what would prove to be the last edition of the festival a couple of months later.

3.

The distinctive mud-brick city of Timbuktu grew up at the crossroads of Tuareg trade routes around 1100. Soon it became the center of the Malian empire. Around this period, an oral constitution known as the Manden Charter became one of the first expressions of civil rights and laws in the world, contemporaneous with the Magna Carta. The Djinguereber Mosque and other buildings made from dried mud established Timbuktu as a center of learning that, in the fourteenth century, was home to twenty-five thousand students.

The empire of Mali arguably reached its peak during the age of Musa, the ninth mansa, or emperor, who reigned from 1312 to 1337. It was a bountiful era for the gold and salt mines around Timbuktu. When Musa set off on his hajj to Mecca, he traversed Africa with an entourage of about sixty thousand people, including twelve thousand slaves, five hundred of whom reputedly carried several pounds of gold. Musa's reputation as the wealthiest man ever to have lived was formed upon his arrival in Cairo, then one of the largest cities in the world. Legend has it that Musa went on such a spending spree that he caused a bout of inflation and a spike in the price of gold that lasted a generation.

Musa's reign was characterized by Sufism, a form of Islam that is often communicated through music, poetry, and art. A caste of musicians flourished, and many of the instruments still played in the Sahel were developed during this era. Over the centuries, Timbuktu scholars produced one of the world's most extensive collections of manuscripts, many of them celebrated for their calligraphy. The jelis, meanwhile, recorded history and customs in songs that were passed down through generations. Periodically, music and manuscript production was interrupted or threatened by more conservative Islamic rulers, who decried any form of artistic representation.

The push and pull between creative expression and religious repression continues to this day. When the jihadists took over northern Mali in 2012, reactionary extremism took hold once again. A former musician named Iyad Ag Ghaly and his jihadist group, called Ansar Dine, imposed sharia law on the region. And true to the tradition of frustrated artists who gain political power, Ghaly attacked art as degenerate.

Fortunately, many of the calligraphic treasures of Timbuktu had already been protected. Joshua Hammer's book *The Bad-Ass Librarians of Timbuktu* describes how, beginning around 2000, librarian Abdel Kader Haidara sailed up and down the Niger, knocking on doors and negotiating personally with village chiefs and private collectors to collate the treasures that were hidden under floorboards and stacked in sheds. Haidara initially housed the collection in museums and libraries around Timbuktu, but spirited them away to Bamako, in a bold escape, when Ghaly took control of the historic city.

The violence has also had a direct effect on Malian music, said Paul Chandler, the music preservationist. When the jihadists occupy towns, music is outlawed, and these laws are enforced brutally. Many local musicians have to go underground.

"They grow beards," Chandler said, "go through all the motions. They would still maybe rehearse but very much in private."

Chandler's nonprofit, Instruments 4 Africa, has spent several years trying to jump-start the music scene by organizing small festivals in areas that have suffered under the jihadist occupation. Along with a team of Malian colleagues, he travels around the north, making sure musicians have the instruments they need to play. But the jihadists are ever-present.

Along with Chandler, Vieux is engaged in a campaign to protect Malian music. He travels to Niafunké and other areas with uncertain security to play at the events organized by Chandler. At the home studio he built during the pandemic and named for his father, Vieux records young traditional musicians. And at the Festival Ali Farka Touré—an annual event intended to replicate the international appeal of the Festival au Désert in the relative safety of the Bamako region—he showcases these acts. The only time I heard him raise his voice and grow excited during our interviews was when he discussed the perilous future of Malian traditional music. He sounded like Volodymyr Zelensky, talking about the survival of a culture he loved, a culture under siege.

Whenever possible, Vieux attempts to give work to musicians who have fled the north. In 2015, Muhamed Dicko started a band in his home of Mopti, another area the jihadists have tried to keep under their thumb. When the band went on tour, Dicko would hide his guitar under luggage in the van, in case they were stopped at improvised rebel roadblocks. Eventually, Dicko said, somebody denounced him because he played at a campaign event for Soumaïla Cissé, a less radical politician who was eventually kidnapped. This time, Dicko's van was singled out at a checkpoint. Dicko credits his survival to the fact that the man who searched the van was a fellow Tamasheq speaker. He promptly fled the region, moving to Bamako.

Unfortunately, the challenges that Malian musicians face are growing worse. In 2020, Assimi Goïta staged the first of a series of coups that have swept through French-speaking Africa. Goïta's unelected "transition" government demanded that the French military, which had kept the jihadists at bay in the north of the country, evacuate. Eventually, the UN peacekeeping forces were asked to leave too. In the last four years, Burkina Faso, Sudan, Niger, and Gabon have all fallen into the hands of military leaders. All the coups appear to have a similar motivation: to drive out the French, whom the juntas often deride as clinging to the vestiges of their empire at the expense of Africans. Most observers say there's some truth to this. For example, France issues the West African CFA franc and

the Central African CFA franc, ensuring stability in the local currencies by pegging them to the euro, in return for economic sway. The problem is that Goïta and others have invited Russia in to fill the vacuum left by the French and international forces. The mercenaries of Russia's state-funded Wagner Group army are treating Malian civilians far more brutally than the French or UN ever did.

People living in the semidesert regions of Mali are now caught in an unenviable position. Jihadists might come to a village in the desert and pressure the locals to become more observant. To avoid persecution, the local men might grow out their beards. When the Wagner Group shows up, they treat anyone with a beard as a jihadist supporter. In 2023 alone, Russian mercenaries have burned down entire villages, killing dozens or possibly hundreds of civilians, including women and children, according to a report from *The Economist* magazine.

Vieux is trying to save his father's music, but the political forces at work are vast. And their effects on the cultural life of the region are already being felt. These days, Vieux has trouble finding people to play more unusual instruments, like the monochord or even the more common bolon, a traditional battle harp.

"Mali is a country for music," said Vieux. "Music is how people learn life, learn history, learn everything. Now the music is coming down."

4.

On one of my last days at the Sleeping Camel, the bar and hotel co-owned by Phil Paoletta, the staff built a stage from overturned milk crates and plywood, in front of the pool. The Camel has no signs on the front of the building anymore, for security reasons. (Bamako has mostly been spared the violence elsewhere in the country, but two deadly attacks in 2015 targeting foreign nationals have led people to take precautions.) The hotel rooms surround a beer garden that is overhung by mango trees, where, as Phil's bird-spotting son Andre will tell you, gray western plantain-eaters often land. On the walls are murals of a shades-wearing camel on a scooter; of a gray western plantain-eater; and of Ali Farka Touré.

"Here is like my house," said Vieux.

The Camel is a home away from home for many wanderers. This is where the people who bring food and medicine to the blockaded city of Timbuktu come to relax. Edouard, a tireless Swiss road warrior, had heard of the Camel from thousands of miles away. When he finally arrived, Phil let him pitch a tent on the patio where Andre and his friends take jujitsu lessons.

Edouard was going to stay only a couple of nights, until he heard about the Vieux Farka Touré gig. While he waited, Edouard sent his goddaughter a postcard, one of more than one hundred he'd dispatched to her during his years of traveling.

Vieux knows everyone at the Camel, and everyone knows him. And yet when he arrives, Vieux cannot relax until the first chords ring out. Onstage, Vieux has a very calm demeanor. But offstage, I came to learn, Vieux is often more harried. After one gig, I tried to interview him and he put up his hand.

"The pressure," he said.

Collaboration is a compulsion for Vieux. The only person he could make time for as he got the stage ready was Juan Carlos Araujo. Araujo, who worked for the UN military mission in Mali, plays Latin jazz. The two men took out their diaries to coordinate the jam session.

"Mali is always like this," Vieux said. "We share our music. It's like an exchange. A musical exchange, a cultural exchange."

As ever, Vieux was well dressed. One of the first times I met him, he was wearing a purple shirt and a bolero tie with an unusual square clasp featuring a horse and a cross. Over the shirt, he wore a pale blue suit with a checked pattern so exquisite, I confess that I googled secondhand ones afterward. On this night, he was wearing a silver diadem in the shape of the African continent, hanging over a crisp pinstriped shirt.

After he took the stage, Vieux lost little time in including guitarist Bady Ag Agaly, who is married to the photographer for this story, Annie Risemberg. Bady himself is another refugee from the wild north, and another Malian musician whose career has been helped by his appearance on a Vieux record.

As the band began to play, I recognized some of the songs they had rehearsed during my first meeting with Vieux. Dicko was back in the groove, singing from his gut, showing the crowd how to let the music take you in its sway like a river. The energy built— that ineffable kinetic power that passes from the players to the dancers and back to the players.

The seats were set up, and a small dance floor. Most people just wigged out near the bar. Strangers danced with strangers. The joy of Vieux's voice was still cut with a kind of sadness. It burrowed its way into the heart. By the end of the show, the entire audience was transported.

For the final song, Vieux played "Na Maïmouna Poussaniamba," which is akin to an African polka. He called out, "Hey!" The guitar and n'goni riffs grew steadily faster with each loop, like fairground rides just after takeoff. The crowd whooped, charged the dance floor, and almost charged the pool, pumping their fists in the air. The song grew faster. Still, the crowd whooped and danced more freely. You could see the legacy of Ali, and of the generations before him, pulsing through the room. Vieux was playing for his people, but more than that he was side by side with his people. I thought about what he'd once told me about Ali. He was driving me back to the Camel from his house. Around us, Bamako was all go: the motorbikes streaming past one another at full speed through every crossroads.

"My father used to be a friend for everybody," he said. "Whether they're kids, women, old people. He was on the same level as everybody." ★

PJ HARVEY

[MUSICIAN, WRITER]

"YOU COME UP WITH ALL SORTS OF CRAZY THINGS
THAT YOU CAN NEVER GET OUT OF YOUR SYSTEM."

Dorset words found in PJ Harvey lyrics, and their English translations:
Drisk (a fine wind-driven mist)
Twiddick (a small twig)
Chilver (a ewe lamb)
Wordle (world)

Polly Jean Harvey is an artist in a constant state of evolution. Those who signed up for the PJ Harvey Fan Club after hearing 1992's volcanic album Dry have happily gone along for the ride as she tries on new styles (music, clothes) and new moods (raucous, melancholic, ecstatic). Few artists can hold on to a devoted fan base no matter whether they are fashioning a folk tale (1995's "Down by the Water"), embracing full-throated politics (2011's Let England Shake), or playing the hurdy-gurdy (2016's The Hope Six Demolition Project). This last effort was a vast multimedia project that included an album recorded behind one-way glass in Somerset House in London, as the public looked on, and was followed by a volume of poems, a collection of photographs, and a Seamus Murphy–directed film, A Dog Called Money, which documented the making of the record. It was a leveling up, but also just another stepping stone for the enigmatic artist in *her continual reinvention, in which she somehow always stays just so fucking cool.*

What's clear, though, is that her creativity cannot be contained in one medium. In addition to her ten studio albums, she crafted the score for the series Bad Sisters, *and her songs were heavily featured on the soundtrack for the second season of* Peaky Blinders. *She's published two books of poetry: 2015's* The Hollow of the Hand *and 2022's* Orlam, *an ambitious book-length poem written after studying with Scottish poet Don Paterson and learning the dialect of her home county. Dorset is located on the coast of England, and is not only where Harvey grew up and currently resides, but also home to the nineteenth-century poet William Barnes, who wrote in the Dorset dialect and inspired* Orlam. *The not exactly autobiographical poem is set there, albeit in an imaginary village called Underwhelem. It follows nine-year-old Ira-Abel and her guardian, Orlam, an all-seeing lamb's eyeball. Despite its strangeness, it is a surprisingly relatable and absorbing volume. Harvey doesn't seem quite ready to leave that place behind. Her 2023 album,* I Inside the Old Year Dying, *takes listeners deeper into the world of* Orlam *while simultaneously exploring intimate landscapes and enormous topics like love and connection. We chatted via Zoom (camera off) about music, language, ghosts, and the correct order for cream and jam on scones.*

—*Melissa Locker*

I. "THE GIFT IS THAT IT BECOMES YOURS"

THE BELIEVER: Last year I went to Sweden to listen to a geo-locked ghost story that you can hear only in the Swedish woods, and it made me think about how important place is when you're listening to things. I was reminded of that with your album. I feel like Dorset is kind of a character in the album and in the poetry book, or at least greatly influences it. Do you think that's true?

PJ HARVEY: Everyone feels differently about things, don't they? But speaking personally, when I am reading a book or listening to a piece of music, I tend to put my own place on it, depending on what I'm feeling. And I think, with regards to the album *I Inside the Old Year Dying*, or even the book *Orlam*, I would hope the reader or the listener situates it in the place that feels right for them and their lives. So for me, it doesn't have to specifically be about Dorset. It could be anywhere, really. I wanted it to be a universal place to come into, and then you just bring your own landscape in with you.

BLVR: Do you think that people who listen in Dorset, or those who are really familiar with the place, might get a different sense of the work than someone living elsewhere?

PJH: Not necessarily. I mean, a lot of the people that live in Dorset don't know the Dorset dialect. I might as well have been writing in a different language altogether, or making up a language, some of which I did, in fact. I think it's open to anyone to come in and engage with the book or the album. The album is not about anything specific in terms of place. It's a much more universally themed album about love and loss and childhood, and searching for meaning in life—as we all try to do. Love itself is the overarching theme.

BLVR: You wrote some of your poems and lyrics in the Dorset language. Is this something you have always known, or is it something you had to go and learn?

PJH: I had to go and learn it. I knew a few words from childhood. I remember some of the older people in the village speaking it. But I had to really go and learn and study. It came to me quite easily, maybe because it was in my blood somewhere, I don't know. But then I think a lot of the words, the sounds of them are quite sensical, if you know what I mean. They sound like what they are, so they're quite easy to remember.

BLVR: Oh yes, like I can almost understand Dutch after I've had a drink. Where does one learn Dorset? Who was your teacher?

PJH: William Barnes. The great William Barnes, long dead, but still probably the greatest poet in the Dorset language, other than Thomas Hardy. He was a poet from the 1800s, and he went about collecting the Dorset-dialect words into a dictionary, I think because he foresaw that it was going to die out. And he wrote in dialect himself. He was also a preacher and walked from town to town preaching. Quite a character. There still exist some beautiful photographs of him in the Dorset Museum.

BLVR: I'm going to guess you were not taught by a ghost, so did you learn from his books?

PJH: From the books, yes, which you can still get in print.

BLVR: It sounds really difficult to learn a whole language that way.

PJH: Well, my lyrics and poems, they're not entirely in dialect. There's a lot of regular, recognizable English words in there. You don't have to know the Dorset dialect to know what's going on. It's more just reaching for a deeper, guttural sort of beauty that I find in them. But also I so love listening to songs in languages I don't understand. I listen to a lot of music from foreign countries that I find utterly beautiful. I don't feel I need to understand the language to feel its beauty and be very moved by it. On the other hand, there's a lot of English singer-songwriters who I often can't understand what they're saying, and I kind of make it up in my head anyway. So I don't think it really matters. If the emotion is there, it's there and you feel it.

BLVR: I always mishear lyrics and kind of love it!

PJH: I love making it up myself. You know, you come up with all sorts of crazy things that you can never get out of your system.

BLVR: Yes, and I love speaking with artists and finding out that I've completely misinterpreted one of their songs for years.

PJH: Yes, but that's the beauty of it, I think. The gift is that it becomes yours. It becomes the listeners'. It becomes the readers'. And you make it your own. And as an artist, I love letting go of it. I wrote the song in the way I understood it, and then I let go. And it doesn't matter, because however it comes across to other people is absolutely right, whatever they find in it.

BLVR: Oh, that's beautiful, and I'm glad to know some people don't mind that.

PJH: Not at all. I think the most beautiful part of listening to music is making it your own, hearing what you hear in it.

BLVR: Do you feel like by working in the Dorset dialect, you were working to preserve it? Do you feel at all like you needed to preserve it?

PJH: Yes. That was on my mind as well: trying to preserve this beautiful language that comes from a very specific, very small area of the world. And if I could do my part to somehow keep a record of that, then I wanted to. And it feels really good now, having *Orlam* out there, having *I Inside the Old Year Dying* out there in the world, because those things will live on after I'm dead and gone, and after the dialect's dead and gone. They'll still be there and people will still go back and find it.

BLVR: You also mentioned that you made up some of your own words.

PJH: Yes, that's right. I think it's a writer's prerogative. If you can't find the word you need, make it up. That's how language comes into being, right?

BLVR: That's true. I mean, think about the word *amaze-balls*, which did not exist at all a few years ago.

PJH: [*Laughs*] Right. And where would we be without that word?

II. "THE BLACK HOLE SAYS IT ALL"

BLVR: I feel like the supernatural comes up a lot in *Orlam*, and I was just curious: Do you believe in ghosts?

PJH: I definitely feel there's something beyond our usual comprehension as human beings. There's something beyond

67

SACRO BOSCO

by Megan Fernandes

After you left, I put on the Pixies,
lit a cigarette and looked out at the rain
on the slate rooftops of Lazio, grey, riddled
with satellites and slanted, orange cranes,
imagined you ascending, shakily,
into a ring of black clouds and thought
of yesterday's sky, blue and bare, stretching
over a park of monsters, where we read Jack's poems
to each other, pausing, roused, while the bronze
hands of Ceres cupped a cobweb like a secret fate,
metal meeting silk, a long-dead sculptor
with a spider's frown. We made no eye contact all day,
kept staring ahead, as if a film were playing
in the near distance, captivating, and easier
to look at because it had nothing to do with us.
Walking home, dark city, along the river, unsteady in my heels
like a drunk gazelle, I heard you say *take my arm*.
And in the morning, you went down
the stairs, paused, then said *I love you*,
and when I didn't answer, you turned, tall, suited
in a stiff jacket, green-eyed, insisted I say it back,
standing firm, more stern than I have ever heard
you, thrilling, and so I said it, impish, then weak,
and kept saying it at the top of the landing
even after you closed the heavy door
and wound down five flights, unable to stop.
I recovered like the pro that I am.
I had the whole apartment to myself.
I had the whole city, cast for my suffering.
Black cloud. Rain. Smoke. Woody smell.
I caught my flight. I changed this poem.
I rode home.

---

my understanding, which I occasionally get glimpses of. It's hard to say, isn't it? When I think of the times in our lives, in human beings' lives, when we feel like everything just stops and changes—at a death, at a birth, at a near-death experience—I feel like there's almost a portal that opens up where you can see there's something more than this, more than our usual day-to-day understanding. I think I've got to glimpse that realm at certain times in my life, during those moments of great transformation that we all go through at some point. But there are also other times that can be transformative for me. Like when you're in the act of creation, in the act of playing, in the act of singing, or in an act of great peace or meditation, then you might also get a glimpse of these things. Or when you're simply being overwhelmed by natural beauty. If you're at a place of unbelievable natural beauty, like standing at the edge of the Grand Canyon or something, you get these little portals where you realize there's more than this. So going back to ghosts: yeah, I think absolutely there's more than what we usually see in our day-to-day lives.

BLVR: I fully agree. Also, it would be so boring to live in a world where we're the only things.

PJH: I think there's so much more that we lost along the way in our development. I don't know, but I think the more in touch we are with nature and with the root of our arrival, the more we are in touch with that other realm, which has a greater understanding, a greater spirituality and sensitivity.

BLVR: Here in the US, Congress just had hearings on aliens, and it's now in the Congressional Record that aliens are probably real, and we're probably not the only ones. I just find it so interesting.

PJH: I heard that, too, and, likewise, I found it interesting. Lately I've been extremely fascinated by black holes and the universe. If you've ever gone looking into black holes deeply, oh my gosh. I mean, talk about mind-boggling.

BLVR: Yes. They're so weird.

PJH: It kind of links into what we're saying, though. The end is the beginning. The beginning is the end. That's another theme of *Orlam*. But there you go. The black hole says it all.

BLVR: It's also so lonely to think we are the only things in the entire universe.

PJH: Yes. It doesn't make much sense, does it? When you think of how big the universe is, to think that we are the only sort of intelligent life form here.

BLVR: Have you ever watched *The X-Files*?

PJH: Yes.

BLVR: The star David Duchovny was at a benefit event recently, and someone asked him about aliens. He shared his theory that aliens send us the perverts only because so many people have alien abduction stories that involve getting probed, and I just love that idea.

PJH: [*Laughs*]

BLVR: I feel like black holes are more mysterious than intergalactic perverts. When you're reading things about space or the universe, do you feel like all that can inform your work?

PJH: Everything I come across that's new all somehow goes into the well of me. And that might turn around and come out as a piece of work at some point.

BLVR: How do you go about learning new things? Is it just that something piques your interest and you go explore it?

PJH: It's hard to explain. I feel drawn to things quite naturally and just sort of follow where I feel I need to look in quite a natural way. It's not preplanned, premeditated. And usually one book or one thing I've read leads to another, leads to another. Same with programs I might have watched, or documentaries or exhibitions I've seen. It's following one's intuition, gut instinct, and just following where it takes you.

BLVR: Do you listen to the radio?

MC Hammer

PJH: I listen to a lot of radio. I listen to a lot of internet radio because you can find some really out-there stations that play the most unusual music. That's actually where I get a lot of my inspiration from, and that's where I find a lot of new artists I want to explore. But there are also some wonderful radio programs here in the UK, particularly on Radio 6 and Radio 3, that you find late at night. There are often some really unusual channels that play things you'd never find by day. I do a lot of exploration of the radio waves. I keep my ear to the ground. I also read a lot of reviews. I think, Oh, that sounds interesting. Then I'll go and check that out. I see a lot of shows that interest me after reading about them, not knowing anything about the artist. It's not like I do it before my work to find better work. I just enjoy and thrive on learning something new, and therefore I very naturally want to do that.

III. LEARNING FROM THE MASTERS

BLVR: I read that you studied poetry for three years. Did people ever recognize you at school, in your poetry classes?

PJH: If they did, they were very polite about not saying so. I think also in those situations, people are there to learn. We're all there for the same reason. It's a great leveling base, so it doesn't really matter. We're all there just to study.

BLVR: How did you choose your poetry teacher?

PJH: Well, he chose me, really. Don Paterson is a wonderful poet from Scotland. He actually came to one of the poetry classes I was a member of and did a weekend workshop in London. I got to meet him there, and we exchanged some poems. He liked my work and offered to help me edit some of it. Through that editing, I realized what an amazing teacher he was, and we became friends. Then he offered to help edit my first book, *The Hollow of the Hand*. After we'd worked on that together, he offered me a mentorship course. Don was teaching at [University of] St. Andrews at the time—he often took on two or three mentorship courses a year—where he would really watch over the shoulder of a poet as they developed their practice. He offered me that mentorship course, and I said yes.

BLVR: How does a poetry mentorship course work? Would he give you a topic or subject, or do you just go and write?

PJH: It's really like being back in the university-degree situation, where you have a lot of study work, a lot of set reading. You have a lot of set tasks to do and poems to write. You hand in your work and then you meet with your teacher and you look up what worked, what didn't work, what you could do better. I'd have lectures on the evolution of poetry over the last one hundred, two hundred years or so. Things like that.

BLVR: I assume you were living at home and you didn't have to go live on campus in a dorm?

PJH: I was at home, but Don and I would meet in London or Scotland.

BLVR: And he would give you homework?

PJH: Yeah, lots of homework. We did very little by Zoom, which was refreshing to me. We'd often meet in person, in real time, and we'd have, like, a four-hour session together. And then, in between times, I'd send him poems through the internet to look at. And then he would look at them and send them back.

BLVR: I admit I basically dropped out of art school because I didn't like being told that paintings or drawings were wrong. I don't like feeling that personal expression is wrong or that you should be graded on it. So how did that work for you? Would he give you critiques? Would he say, *Oh no, that's completely incorrect. Use this word instead?*

PJH: I think you can be told that in poetry, or in any art form, actually, it's a craft and you need to learn it. You learn from the greats. You learn from the masters. You learn from the teachers that have gone before you. You can have your personal voice, but you still need to learn the craft. It's no good just having a personal voice and writing in a not-very-good way. There's a lot to be learned from study, hard work, study.

BLVR: Would he have you read only the great poets, or would he also have you read really mediocre ones so you could learn, *Don't do that?*

PJH: He had me read a lot of work, and some of it was not good work, so I could see why it wasn't good. In critiquing

my own work, he'd really explain why what I was doing was not as good as it could be, and he'd show me how it could be better. And I found that really enthralling and exciting. I never took it as a slight upon myself. It was always just very exciting to see how I could improve.

BLVR: Did you ever have to write a rhyming poem?

PJH: Many times, yes. You can get a lot across in a rhyming poem because the rhyme somehow already ties it up and makes it seem right. So you can say all sorts of wrong things in a poem that rhymes, and people will still think you're right.

IV. TANDEM WORK

BLVR: In addition to poetry and your own music, you've also been doing a lot of musical scoring. That was a terrible segue. Just go with it.

PJH: [*Laughs*] Yeah. I really enjoy working with visual images or in theater. I love working with actors. I have so much respect for them. I love working with directors—theater, film, TV directors. So it's an absolute joy. I'd love to do more because it's lovely to collaborate and to be one part of a whole, of making something great if you can.

BLVR: How do you approach working from a visual image versus creating your own album from scratch? How do you approach scoring?

PJH: If we're talking about film and TV, it's good to have the information about the scene. It's quite good to know the script and to know what's happened before and after. It's quite good to chat with the director about what they're wanting to capture at that moment in time, or what they're wanting to capture in the overall soundtrack. You have to have quite a lot of talk beforehand with the directors about that. I really enjoy trying to meet their wishes, because it makes me explore areas of my own composition that I probably wouldn't have gone into otherwise.

BLVR: Are there directors you'd like to work with?

PJH: Oh yes, many. I hope that will happen one day, but I

think that also comes from the work you've done. People see what you have done, and if they like it, they might reach out.

BLVR: How did you come to work on *Bad Sisters*?

PJH: Sharon Horgan reached out to me, and I said yes before I saw anything, because I'm a huge fan of her work, always have been. I always want to follow what she's doing. So that was a great thrill. And we've just started talking about *Bad Sisters 2*, so that's more excitement in the future.

BLVR: Who are they going to kill this time?

PJH: I'm not telling you.

BLVR: Fair. Sharon Horgan is one of those actors who… I just want her to be my friend.

PJH: Yeah, you would, because she's a terrific person and she's lovely to be around. And she is very funny.

BLVR: Typical. Going back to other directors, do you want to name some names? Maybe we can manifest working with them for you?

PJH: I don't know. That feels a bit… I don't want to be trying to say, *Work with me! Work with me!* But I have some favorite filmmakers. People like Paul Thomas Anderson, or Yorgos Lanthimos, Jonathan Glazer, Quentin Tarantino, Céline Sciamma. I could go on. Jane Campion. Joanna Hogg. I love their work, but I think what will be, will be. Directors have to choose the right composer for the type of film they're making. And a lot of those directors I've just named already have really great relationships with composers. I can understand that they would want to keep working with those people. You know, Jon Glazer works with Mica Levi a lot. Paul Thomas Anderson works with Jonny Greenwood, et cetera, et cetera.

BLVR: Oh! I've interviewed Mica. They're amazing, but now I'm concerned I've mispronounced their name.

PJH: I'm never sure quite how to pronounce their name. I think it's Mica? I'm not sure.

BLVR: I thought it was Mica.

PJH: You're right: it's Mica. Mica Levi.

BLVR: Well, this is print, so we will not be setting the record straight here. Do you feel like that's a direction you'd like to go in your career, just doing more…

PJH: More soundtrack work?

BLVR: Yeah. Thank you for finishing my sentence.

PJH: I see it in tandem with my own songwriting work and my poetry work. It's not like something I want to just go into from now on. I see it as part of some of the other things I do, and I'm always open to it.

MICROINTERVIEW WITH VICTOR OLADIPO, PART VII

THE BELIEVER: Perhaps your most notable solo was at Madison Square Garden during the 2015 Slam Dunk Contest, when you sang Frank Sinatra's "New York, New York" in front of a packed arena—then threw down a nasty reverse 360-degree spin. What was that night like for you, to showcase these skills on the same stage? And how do you maintain your ability to work at both of them?

VICTOR OLADIPO: Honestly, I was nervous about the whole thing, to be real with you, bro. The dunk—that was the first time I'd done it. That was also my first time singing in front of people like Rihanna, Nicki Minaj, Meek [Mill], Spike [Lee]. It was crazy. That was my second year in the league, so I was young and super nervous, but it turned out really good. The singing might have been better than the dunk for me. [*Laughs*] Recently I put a studio in my house. That's exciting because I've never had that. I can just go and make a new song. That's monumental. Home is my base. God willing, it's where I end up every day. So to have that opportunity to be able to just go to my house and create a song? That's different. A stronger connection. I don't have to go far to find that release. I can just go to the back room. ★

BLVR: I have read several interviews with you that make it seem like people sometimes just approach you with things, and you're like, *Oh yeah, that sounds fun. Let's do that.* Do you think that's true?

PJH: No. It has to resonate with me. I'm often asked to contribute to things, but if it doesn't resonate with me, then I politely decline. I only work on things that I feel will have great meaning for me, and that I can therefore find moving and contribute some good work to.

V. CREAM FIRST, JAM SECOND

BLVR: I feel like people sometimes forget that you're a real person and instead think of you as Artist PJ Harvey, an image. But you go to class, you watch Quentin Tarantino movies, you're very much a real person as well. Do you feel like people forget sometimes?

PJH: I think that's something we all do. I think I do the same with great artists that I love. You don't often imagine they do those small things that we all have to do, but yeah, I'm just a regular person. I really am.

BLVR: It seems like you're also very good at boundaries. You don't do very many interviews, and after this one I'm sure you'll never do another. Do you feel like that separation between performance and the personal is important for you?

PJH: That's a difficult one to answer, because I don't feel like I become different people. I'm still Polly whether I'm performing or whether I'm with a friend or reading a book at home, you know? I don't feel like I become a different person. At the same time, I guess what you're asking about is boundaries, and I do protect myself. I know when I'm overreaching, when I need to draw back a bit and have some quiet time.

BLVR: What do you do in your free time? It sounds like you have so many interests. And how do you distinguish between work research and learning just for fun?

PJH: They all sort of teach each other because I have fun just learning. You could say it's all research—every book I read, every exhibition I see. It doesn't feel like I'm going out and doing hard study. But it's hard work. You have to really put in the hours. And I do that. I'm a very conscientious worker and I work hard to create the works that I have. But then the things that might inform them are quite joyful for me to do—like practicing scales, or learning new chords, trying to get better at the piano, reading about things I never knew about, watching documentaries. It's that part I enjoy. It's hard work, but I enjoy it too.

BLVR: Oh, I agree. I love learning things. Like I just learned how to fix a broken sink, and now I want to learn more.

PJH: It's very rewarding, too, isn't it? When you learn how to do something practical like that, you really feel you've achieved something.

BLVR: Are you on TikTok at all?

PJH: Yes.

MICROINTERVIEW WITH VICTOR OLADIPO, PART VIII

THE BELIEVER: What does *TUNDE* represent for you at this stage in your career?

VICTOR OLADIPO: I've gone through a lot dealing with injuries. You go from people loving you and you feeling that love, and when you get hurt it can go away a little bit. You pay attention to who really loves you the way you want to be loved. I'm hyperaware that I've always gotten love from my people: Nigerians, Africans of every descent, culture, background. I want to give them that same love and respect. So I did an Afrobeats album and I named it *TUNDE* because my name [in Yoruba] is Babatunde, which means "dad come back." It was my first album since 2018. It felt very fitting. Afrobeats is like a new version of R&B, a new wave. I was in the studio with one of my producers and he said we should create a new genre called Fro'n'B [a mix of Nigerian Afrobeats and American R&B]. It seemed like a perfect fit. My project was going toward that. Showing love to my people, my country, the continent of Africa. ✲

BLVR: I love TikTok because it is filled with useful skills that I did not know I needed.

PJH: Yeah, yes.

BLVR: What does the TikTok algorithm give you? Like what videos show up?

PJH: Well, like you said, I think it's a place to immediately get any information that you want in a very simple way. And that's good for me.

BLVR: Yeah. I love recipes. I love dog videos. I'll take any of them. Are you on other social media?

PJH: Yes.

BLVR: And do you enjoy it or do you find it sort of a time suck? Both?

PJH: Both. I think we can all get sucked into that, can't we? And you have to kind of draw yourself out of it again. But I think it's also a great place to find information. And it's good to see what other people are doing. I don't think of it as a bad thing at all. Obviously, there are some things that are bad on it. I'm not referring to that.

BLVR: Do you have any guilty pleasures?

PJH: Guilty pleasures? I can't think of anything. If I think of anything, I'll let you know. I probably do and I'm just not going to tell you.

BLVR: That is fair. I mean, not everyone needs to know about your addiction to *Forensic Files,* right? Is there anything else you'd like to talk about?

PJH: Um. Ooh.

BLVR: Ah, now I made your brain go blank. Perfect.

PJH: Now we're going to be silent before the end of it. Well, I'm just looking forward to playing some shows. We're about to go out on tour through Europe with *I Inside the Old Year*

Dying, and we'll be coming to the States next year. Really looking forward to that and to now being able to actually meet and perform with people.

BLVR: Because you're from Dorset, do you believe in putting jam on your scone first, then cream—or cream, then jam?

PJH: I think I'm a cream, then jam kind of person.

BLVR: Really? That seems so difficult. Doesn't the cream just squish everywhere?

PJH: No, no. You kind of have to hold it so the jam doesn't run off. But that's all part of the fun and enjoyment.

BLVR: That sounds very sticky. Well, I know what my afternoon plans are now.

PJH: But you didn't ask about Dorset apple cake, did you?

BLVR: What is Dorset apple cake?

PJH: I think it kind of supersedes the scone.

BLVR: Really? OK.

PJH: Probably the most Dorset dish. Yeah.

BLVR: Well, I bet they have a recipe on TikTok.

PJH: Probably. ✶

Missy Elliott

IN SEARCH OF WHOLENESS

with

BTS

HOW JUNG'S IDEA OF THE "SHADOW SELF" INSPIRED THE WORLD'S BIGGEST K-POP GROUP

by

MIMI LOK

illustrations by

MADISON KETCHAM

In the West, people just don't get it. Korea is a country that has been invaded, razed to the ground, torn in two. Just seventy years ago, there was nothing. But now the whole world is looking at Korea. How is that possible? How did that happen? Because people try so fucking hard to better themselves. You are in France or the UK, countries that have been colonizing others for centuries, and you come to me with: *Oh god, you put so much pressure on yourselves; life in Korea is so stressful!* Well, yes. That's how you get things done. And it's part of what makes K-pop so appealing, although, of course, there's a dark side. Anything that happens too fast and too intensely has side effects.

—RM, leader of BTS

No noble, well-grown tree ever disowned its dark roots, for it grows not only upward but downward as well.

—Carl Gustav Jung, founder of analytical psychology

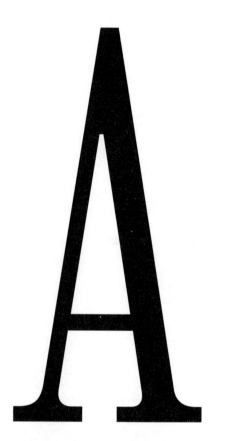

A long time ago, before I was a writer, before I was an ardent fan of the K-pop group BTS, I was an undergraduate art student. I spent my days in a cold building in the northeast of England manipulating photographs, wax, muslin, paint, collages, and knives. I was making work about memory and identity, and, somewhat

76

appropriately, spent much of my time groping around in the dark, figuratively and literally—developing photographs in a darkroom, or experimenting with slide projections in an abandoned university administrative office I'd claimed for myself. I can't remember what I took so many photographs of, only that I'd enlarge and blur them, then cut out details, and mummify them in squares of wax melted into long muslin rectangles that I then hung from the ceiling like fly strips or funereal party streamers.

At the time I was influenced by the work of the artist Christian Boltanski, specifically his installation works spanning the late '80s and '90s that he made, in his words, not "about the Holocaust but *after* the Holocaust," and, more broadly, on the themes of loss and individual and collective memory. These haunting works often featured stark altar-like arrangements of re-photographed archival portraits, single black-and-white faces enlarged to the point of blurring into extreme chiaroscuro. The portraits were illuminated by bare light bulbs attached to black electrical cords that trailed along the floor of the exhibition space like sleeping Medusa hairs—the mechanics and artifice of these works on full display. To a viewer, this invited an unsettled, constantly shifting experience that alternated in focus between the individual images and the collection of images in concert with one another; between immersive communion with these unknown souls and objective appraisal of the artifact; between light and dark.

These works became the subject of my dissertation, in which I explored their connection to Carl Jung's ideas of the collective unconscious (the idea that a form of the unconscious mind is shared by all humans, and contains the experiences, memories, and knowledge of our ancestors) and the shadow (the unconscious part of the human psyche that contains the rejected, repressed, and unaccepted aspects of ourselves), and the lasting impact of human experiences on the psyche. This dissertation was my first encounter with Jungian thought, and I remember being drawn to the shadow archetype as a way of understanding humankind's propensity toward violence and war and, by the same token, understanding its propensity toward racism. Understanding shadow projection made the experience of racism no less painful. But it was a preferred alternative to the idea that one was deserving of it, and/or that such behavior was inexplicable and therefore without a solution.

I was also deeply attracted to Jung's concept of a collective unconscious and its ties to personal and cultural memory. This collective unconscious is considered to contain archetypal images, or primordial symbols, that are passed down through generations and are common to all human cultures, representing universal truths and patterns. Jung believed that these archetypal images are expressed in dreams, myths, and art and literature, and that they can help us to understand our own lives and the lives of others. He also believed that the collective unconscious could be tapped into and used to positively influence our own behavior.

The notion of an unseen, unifying force linking past and present resonated with me, particularly as someone whose relationship to her heritage was characterized by a persistent feeling of incompleteness, and by a yearning that alternated between hopeless grasping and resignation. I was born and raised in England, to parents who'd immigrated from Hong Kong, and my family was one of two Chinese families in our small, predominantly white town. Growing up, I felt indelibly British in many ways, and yet daily experiences of racism and xenophobia, as well as the paucity of representation—I didn't see myself in books, classroom curricula, or on the screen—undermined my sense of self and my hopes of belonging. At home I ate Chinese food, watched Chinese TV, and listened to Cantopop, but I couldn't speak or read Chinese as well as I wanted to, and I did not grow up with any relatives around—all of them were in Hong Kong. It was only in the pages of books by writers like Maxine Hong Kingston, Gish Jen, and Peter Ho Davies that I found some companionship in my condition of in-betweenness.

I often wondered what it would take to feel complete, to feel whole. Jung's ideas felt almost too good to be true. Did they really contain the answers to life, the universe, and everything? I delved deeper, learning more about his "map of the soul"—his theory of the human psyche—and the interplay of persona (the interface between the individual and society that makes up a person's social identity); ego (the center of consciousness, the "I"); and shadow. I learned that the Jungian definition of *wholeness* is "the emergent sense of psychic complexity and integrity that develops over the course of a complete lifetime." In other words, one must fully accept and integrate every part of oneself, and it takes a bloody long time. I was just scratching the surface, and already I was finding his writings intimidatingly vast, eclectic, and at times bewildering. I felt as if I were getting lost in a darkened, overgrown maze, and it was suffocating.

Something must have happened between my dissertation submission and my degree show, for which graduating students were required to make a culminating work. I did not want to make another monochromatic, funereal piece. Perhaps I was tired of spending so much time in the gray, somber zone. Perhaps I realized it wasn't the only way to talk about memory and identity. For my final piece, I had an ambitious vision of a circus-like tent made of red satin, big enough to hold about fifteen people. Upon entering, you were greeted by a bouncy Mandarin love song from the '60s. As you looked up, you saw a small army of fans made from knife blades hanging in rows from a rotisserie-like contraption, light glinting off the blades as they turned.

Looking back, I find the symbolism of the piece rather heavy-handed. But I admire my then self's thoughtless, enthusiastic seizing of this vision that sprang from my unconscious depths. I was able to pull off that bizarre spectacle thanks to this lack of self-consciousness, as well as an apparent absence of institutional concern for visitor safety. To this day, I'm still deeply relieved that no visitors were harmed by a falling blade.

Art school was followed by years of restless searching. It feels strange to acknowledge that during this decades-long period of roaming across continents, cultures, and professions (I lived in Hong Kong and the States, and worked in the arts, journalism, education, and nonprofit human rights), I

didn't really think about Jung again. It almost feels like a betrayal, to have once been so inspired and moved by something, only to abandon it in favor of other sources of ideas and enrichment. But that is precisely what happened.

Late one evening in February 2020, I come across a YouTube video. The Korean group BTS are performing their new single "ON" at Grand Central Terminal in New York, as part of an appearance on *The Tonight Show Starring Jimmy Fallon*. I've heard of them and have previously seen a few of their performances on US chat shows, though they didn't leave much of an impression. Nevertheless, something makes me click through.

The performance begins in a deserted, after-hours station concourse. A glittering organ intro. A group of unsmiling, black-clad dancers and marching-band members move in stiff synchronicity like a dystopian *Rhythm Nation*–like army. The camera swings low and welcomes an androgynous, blue-haired Asian man in white, who, entering the frame with sinewy, swanlike movements, sings the opening line in a breathy, honeyed voice. He, too, is unsmiling, and projects a looking-down-his-nose-at-you confidence to the camera. He's soon joined by other members of the group, each singing or rapping different lines with the same defiant, intense energy ("Bring the pain!"). The transitions between one member and another are seamless, showcasing their distinct vocals while evoking a gang-like unity. The choreography has the graceful intensity of a John Woo shoot-out or a *Crouching Tiger, Hidden Dragon* fight sequence,

and pulses and transforms at such a dizzying pace that it feels like witnessing a mathematically complex ballet. It ends with the clattering echo of drumsticks hitting the floor, and the seven band members turning their backs to the camera, arms flung protectively around one another's shoulders and waists.

I am speechless, unsure of what I've just witnessed. I replay it a dozen times. I try to learn the part of the choreography that resembles a two-handed, zigzaggy window wash. I send the video to my family group chat, certain that every one of them, from my eighty-something mother to my preteen nephew, will also be awed by the brilliance of it. There are some polite thumbs-ups, but only my choreographer sister expresses her reaction in words: "They're all such good movers! But the blue-haired one dances like he's moving through water."

Later, I contemplate a detail from after the performance ends, when Fallon comes in to thank BTS and wrap up the show. In this moment, the members of BTS drop their tough, intense performance personae and let their total exhaustion show through. One of the members, on the far left, gives a floppy, Muppet-like wave to the camera before succumbing to a comically dramatic collapse. I find it surprising and endearing. In that cheerful collapse, I see a group of dedicated artists who are utterly committed to the performance, and, when it's over, are comfortable with discarding that pristine persona. How fascinating, I think. That's not something you see all the time.

I decide to learn their names. There's RM, the leader, who learned English from watching *Friends* and wanted to be a poet, before he became a rapper. There's Jin, SUGA (also known as Agust D), j-hope, Jimin (the blue-haired one from the "ON" performance), V (the collapsing, Muppet-waving one from the "ON" performance), and Jung Kook. I learn that BTS stands for "Bangtan Sonyeondan," which translates to "Bulletproof Boy Scouts," and also stands for "Beyond the Scene." I learn that "ON" is a single from their latest album, *Map of the Soul: 7*, a Jungian exploration of the self, continued from their previous release, the EP *Map of the Soul: Persona*. Song titles include "Persona," "Interlude: Shadow," and "Outro: Ego." At first, I don't think much of the Jungian references; pop music, after all, frequently draws inspiration from a multitude of sources. But the more I listen, the more I am struck by what a rich journey the album offers, how intimate, transporting, and viscerally affecting the songs are. Framed by an unflinching appraisal of the group's relationship to music, creativity, and fame, the ensemble tracks are complimented by seven solo numbers in which each member reflects on his personal journey. I am impressed by the depth and ambition not just of the album, but also of the associated projects celebrating its release, from the visually rich music videos to the contemporary dance art film commissioned for the album's other title song, "Black Swan," and their global art project, "Connect, BTS," involving twenty-two artists making large-scale art installations on multiple continents. I hear about a book on Jungian psychology, *Jung's Map of the Soul: An Introduction* by Murray Stein, and its reported influence on BTS. I buy it.

At first, I don't think much of the Jungian references; pop music, after all, frequently draws inspiration from a multitude of sources.

Reading about Jung again, more than twenty years later, I feel a halting familiarity and curious apprehension more commonly associated with reconnecting with an old friend, uncertain if we'll still like each other. Perhaps I also feel guilt for not returning his calls.

The tentativeness with which I reacquaint myself with Jung is in stark contrast to my eager tumble down the BTS rabbit hole. I learn that all BTS members are deeply involved in the creation of their music, through a mix of songwriting, producing, choreography, and performance direction. I realize, through watching their many award show and concert performances, that the intricate theatricality of the stage-craft and the blend of old-school charisma and professionalism make me at once nostalgic for the Hong Kong Cantopop concerts I grew up watching in the '80s and thrilled by the genre- and gender-bending innovation of their music and aesthetics. BTS members wear makeup onstage for performances, music videos, and photo shoots, donning skirts, lace, pearl necklaces, et cetera, with great panache, particularly when combined with styling that would be considered more conventionally masculine. Their choreography ranges from intense, synchronized hip-hop movements to an airy, balletic grace. Musically, they glide between genres (hip-hop, R&B, trap, bubblegum dream pop, and rock, to name a few), singing and rapping mostly in Korean with smatterings of English. But what I find particularly exciting is their blending of the traditional and the contemporary that results in something that sounds, and feels, unique. Their 2018 song "IDOL," for example, layers classical Korean instruments over the thumping drum and bass of gqom, a style of house music that originated in Durban, South Africa. SUGA's 2020 solo rap song "Daechwita" is inspired by and samples daechwita, a genre of Korean traditional military music, as well as pansori, a genre of folk-musical storytelling. More and more, they seem to me the epitome of fluidity, building on the possibilities of pop music by combining their cultural past and present while looking to the future.

Something else that feels familiar about BTS—and very Asian—is the deference and gratitude they express to their fans at every possible opportunity (in BTS's case, the diverse, devoted, many-million-strong fan base known as ARMY, an acronym for Adorable Representative M.C. for Youth, a nod to the group's hip-hop idol roots). At first I'm not sure how to receive this earnestness, before (1) remembering that it's a long-held practice among Cantopop singers and Hong Kong actors, including massive stars like Anita Mui and Leslie Cheung back in their day, a common utterance to fans and audiences being "Thank you for your support!"; and (2) learning about BTS's humble underdog origins and their indebtedness to their fans. I discover that BTS started their career with Big Hit, a small management company on the verge of bankruptcy. Unlike the powerful "Big Three" entertainment companies (SM, YG, and JYP) that dominated the K-pop entertainment industry for the past two decades, Big Hit lacked both the money and the influence required to secure media coverage and coveted TV spots for the group. Instead, BTS engaged with their (then considerably smaller) fan base through social media, relying on grassroots support to sustain morale and achieve early success.

Over the following weeks and months, I binge BTS's music videos, reality travel shows, and weekly variety shows; learn their personality quirks; and watch their live streams and tour documentaries. I learn they are extremely funny and self-aware. I forge close friendships over BTS, and get up after midnight to watch their pandemic "at-home" live streamed concerts, during which I exchange excited texts with fellow ARMY friends in other cities. These are rare moments of joyful, intimate communion during an intensely isolating time. Online, I am welcomed into a corner of the ARMYverse and am heartened to learn of many other fans' similar conversions, their own tumbles down the rabbit hole invariably starting with "I'll just learn their names." I realize the closest I've previously come to this level of energizing discovery is when I've been writing the first draft of a story.

During this time, I am also journeying through BTS's vast, eclectic discography on long walks or runs around my neighborhood. It does not surprise me to learn of their socially conscious themes, starting with their earliest work. In their 2013–14 School Trilogy (the first "era" of their career), they speak out against academic pressure in the song "N.O" (the music video shows them leading a classroom revolt) and income inequality in "Spine Breaker" (the music video's DIY camcorder aesthetic reminds me of the satirical, anarchic wit of early Beastie Boys). Their subsequent eras—Most Beautiful Moment in Life Trilogy (2015–16) and Wings (2016–17)—affectingly capture the despair, adventure, and fragile hope of youth and growing up, and in the case of "Spring Day," collective grief over a national tragedy. The song is widely acknowledged as a tribute to the victims of the 2014 *Sewol* ferry disaster, which claimed the lives of over three hundred passengers, most of them high school students, and led to widespread social and political upheaval in the country. The song is beautiful and poignant on its own, but the music video makes the experience of the song richly transcendent, and includes visual references to the movie *Snowpiercer* and Ursula K.

Le Guin's story "The Ones Who Walk Away from Omelas," in which the happiness of a utopian community is dependent on the suffering of a child. In the music video, there's a moment when the members sit on a colorful mountain of clothes. It takes me a moment to realize it's a reference to another monument of memory, loss, and resurrection, by none other than Christian Boltanski. In 2010, Boltanski created large-scale, site-specific installations using tons of discarded clothes in the Grand Palais, in Paris, and in the Park Avenue Armory, in New York. Four hundred thousand items of clothing were heaped into a mountain, with other clothes laid out in the shape of rectangles, turning the space into a cemetery. In Paris, he called it *Personnes*. In New York, he called it *No Man's Land*. While running forward with BTS, I feel like I'm going back in time.

This is not my first experience being part of a fandom. As a kid, I saved up my allowance to buy my first record—a-ha's *Take On Me*. I had the posters, the tour merch, and the fan club magazines, and I went around confidently telling my school friends that (according to singer Morten Harket) gifting a cactus to a Norwegian is a way of telling them they're an asshole. As a teenager I was a massive Cure fan: I went to countless concerts; I had the posters, the tour merch, and the fan club magazines. I could tell you that Robert Smith's favorite beer was Sol, that he liked to drink tea in the bath, and that he took inspiration for one of their songs from a Patrick White short story. Later, I was an avid fan of *Buffy the Vampire Slayer*. I memorized quotes, attempted to write

fan fiction, read the comics, pored over analyses of characters and themes, and delighted in the academic studies that branched out from the fandom. In other words, I was, in theory, built for the BTS ARMY life. But the reality was that nothing could have prepared me for the level of joy, intensity, and comfort that being a BTS fan brings, or for it to be a portal back to Jungian ideas. And to chance upon all this on the brink of a global pandemic—to have the opportunity to cultivate a new source of passion, discovery, and community during a time of isolation and despair—was a truly unexpected gift.

You don't have to be a fan of BTS to recognize the significance of their achievements: as a K-pop group addressing taboo subjects in Korean culture, including mental health issues, and their staunch support of LGBTQ rights; as an Asian group that has broken numerous records and barriers in the Western music industry (the tip of the iceberg: they are the first Grammy-nominated K-pop group, the first to chart a primarily Korean-language single, "Life Goes On," at number one in the United States, and they grossed $230 million in concert revenue in 2022, outstripping Harry Styles and Coldplay; they have also won all four major categories at the Mnet Asian Music Awards for three years in a row); and as representatives for South Korea and Korean culture on the global stage. Since 2017 they've partnered with UNICEF on the Love Myself campaign, an effort to end violence toward children and teens. In 2018 they visited the United Nations, where RM gave a speech on the importance of

finding one's voice. They returned in 2021 as special presidential envoys for South Korea, rejected the labeling of today's youth as the generation "lost to COVID," and instead lauded their resiliency, curiosity, and inclusiveness. After George Floyd was killed, on May 25, 2020, BTS posted a simple message on Twitter condemning racial discrimination and violence and donated $1 million to Black Lives Matter. When explaining their decision behind the donation, SUGA said, "Ours are initiatives that any person who wishes to live in a just world would want to pursue. We aren't trying to send out some grandiose message… It's about us being against racism and violence. Most people would be against these things." Inspired by this act, ARMY—which has a long and diverse track record of philanthropic activity—raised a further $1 million in donations within twenty-four hours.

For me, one of BTS's most meaningful public statements came in the wake of the Atlanta spa shootings on March 16, 2021, in which eight people were killed, six of whom were Asian women.

I was never the same again after that day. It was as if a dam had burst, and all the layered pain of racism, xenophobia, and misogyny I'd been holding on to over decades came rushing out all at once. In the immediate aftermath of the shootings, I struggled to make sense of my visceral anguish, let alone of the world around me, which seemed to exist in a separate reality. Nobody seemed to be talking about Atlanta or reaching out to check in. When I went for a walk, I passed by people discussing their lunch plans or their pets, or where to get a vaccination, and I noticed how

You have received a freebie from me! It's small but I hope it gives you a bit of happiness. Enjoy! <3

we faced discrimination as Asians. We have endured expletives without reason and were mocked for the way we look. We were even asked why Asians spoke in English." They described their experiences as "inconsequential" compared with the Atlanta shooting, but said such incidents "chip away" at their self-esteem. I found their direct way of expressing their feelings, and their willingness to be vulnerable, deeply moving and admirable. During a time of feeling smothered by the silence surrounding this topic, their words felt like a sharp glimmer of light, reflected off a mirror in someone's palm—not an SOS call, but an answer to one: *No, you're not crazy. Yes, it's OK to feel grief and anger. We feel it too.*

I thought about the burden of Asian public figures who are expected to channel their devastation into articulate, digestible sound bites; of Asian journalists tasked with reporting on the news while not having a chance to process their own grief; and of Asian folks in general expected to carry on—at school, at work, at home—as if nothing had happened. I thought about who else might be feeling isolated during this time, who else needed to feel seen.

In the days that followed, I talked with dozens of AAPI friends, acquaintances, and strangers I'd met at vigils and online solidarity gatherings. There was a wide variety of responses, ranging from detachment and numbness to despair and white-hot rage. We talked about how people we trusted and considered close had not reached out or acknowledged the shootings in a timely or adequate way, or at all. We talked about struggling with institutional silence and lack of care that ranged

jarring those business-as-usual words felt in comparison with the overwhelming grief I was experiencing. Online, my feeds were full of the same: by and large, life appeared to go on while I alternated between rage, tears, and disbelief, wondering if there was something wrong with me for having these feelings. The few mentions of Atlanta I did see online came mostly from Asian folks, BTS being the most prominent. In a letter posted to Twitter, the members said they felt "grief and anger," adding: "What our voice must convey is clear. We stand against racial discrimination. We condemn violence." The statement continued, "We recall moments when

A friend of mine, the author Ipek Burnett, wisely told me that "a breakdown can also be a breakthrough."

from making us feel invisible to uncomfortably singling us out as representatives of all AAPIs. We talked about how all this compounded the feelings of isolation we were already holding, which added to the existing layers of pain. We talked about the countless others who must also be going through this and feeling the same way, grieving in the wake of Atlanta and amid the larger wave of anti-Asian violence sweeping the country. We talked about how these latest attacks were part of a long history of injustice toward Asians in myriad forms—from microaggressions and legally sanctioned discrimination to expressions of lethal violence. With all I was bearing witness to, in myself and others, silence no longer felt like an option. I felt I had to do something, no matter how small, to break it.

I drafted a document that began with a brief description of what I and others in the AAPI community were going through, followed by a list of actions and resources. I titled it "8 Things You Can Do to Support the AAPIs in Your Life." It was a way of demanding visibility, offering solace, calling for allyship, and also, I realized, it was a sort of wish list for how I wanted myself and others to be treated, and in the process of writing it, I was confronting the various ways I had learned over a lifetime to suppress and contort myself in order to accommodate others. These contortions were, I think, an example of the antithesis of the wholeness for which a Jungian psychological model advocates. I emailed the document to people who I thought might find it helpful, and also posted it online, not expecting much from the latter, since I am rarely on social media and don't have many followers. But the resource ended up being shared more widely than I ever could have imagined. I received messages from AAPIs saying that they felt validated and seen, and from non-AAPIs who expressed gratitude for the guidance on how to be a better ally. But I was too exhausted to respond. At work, and also for my personal emails, I set up an out-of-office autoresponder explaining that I was taking time for myself in the wake of the shootings and would not be responding to anything that wasn't related to supporting the victims and AAPI communities. I included a link to the "8 Things" document and a list of opportunities for donating or learning more. After that, I turned off my laptop and phone and let my eyes fall shut. I could feel myself crumbling emotionally and physically, and I knew I needed to seek professional help.

I don't recall listening to any music at all at the onset of my mental breakdown. But a little further along in my depression, I turned to BTS's more gentle, introspective tracks on their pandemic album, *BE*, for glimmers of hope and reassurance. And that summer, dealing with a family loss and a difficult move, I played "Let Go" and "Moving On" on a loop to help keep myself going.

A friend of mine, the author Ipek Burnett, wisely told me that "a breakdown can also be a breakthrough." As I set about the work of self-repair, I wondered what it was I was trying to rebuild, and what I had broken through to. I had to ask myself the same question I'd asked half a lifetime before, when I was an undergraduate art student researching Jung: *What does it mean to be whole?* When I thought back to that time, I could picture only my then self in a state of solitude, moving about my art studio late at night or hunched over a slide projector in an abandoned office. I knew I'd immersed myself in the texts and art of others, but I couldn't recall actually talking to anyone about any of this.

This time around, the question of wholeness has felt much different. Through the lens of greater maturity; through meaningful time spent with friends, family, colleagues, my various AAPI communities, ARMYs both Jungian and non-Jungian; through the music of BTS; and through reading books and academic papers and listening to podcasts on mental health and Jungian psychology, this exploration of the self has felt richer and more creative, grounded as much in community and connection with others as it is in solitary reflection.

Essentially, I've become profoundly aware that the search for meaning, for wholeness—indeed, the *experience of becoming whole*—cannot happen in isolation. It requires interaction with those around me and with their ideas, and witnessing what these interactions illuminate inside of me, to bring clarity to my own thoughts and feelings.

In light of all this, I knew I wanted to start working on this piece by talking to other people about their relationship to BTS and Jung. My love of BTS is deeply entwined with a love of community, and it felt like a unique opportunity to learn about the different ways members of these communities draw their own meaning and joy from each, in turn enriching my own appreciation and understanding.

It is also very much informed by my work at Voice of Witness (VOW), the nonprofit organization I cofounded almost fifteen years ago that uses oral history to amplify the voices of people marginalized by race-, gender-, and class-based inequity. VOW's work—its book series, education programming, and community engagement efforts—takes a polyphonic, first-person narrative approach to gaining a nuanced understanding around human rights issues. In other words, if you want to learn about something, first talk to the people with direct experience of it, people whose lives are deeply shaped by it.

I'll confess to another reason I wanted to conduct interviews for this essay: When I was first asked to write this piece, my initial reaction was giddy excitement at the prospect of delving more deeply into BTS and Jungian psychology, swiftly followed by abject terror at the prospect of writing a personal essay for publication. I have a long-held aversion to writing directly about myself; I've generally preferred to dwell in the realms of fiction and oral history, where fictional characters or real-life narrators take center stage, not myself, and why I've often felt a timorous admiration of certain memoirists comparable to my admiration of base jumpers: *Wow, impressive, good for them, but*

nope, absolutely not for me, thank you. Some of that has to do with my private nature, some of it with my complicated, evolving relationship to vulnerability. So, much as I did in the aftermath of the Atlanta spa shootings (and in the aftermath of more recent violence in Monterey Park and Half Moon Bay, California), and much as I've been doing in my broader work toward wholeness, I looked to others to find the courage and clarity that were lacking in myself. Indeed, it was only after many hours of conversations with Jungians, ARMYs, and Jungian ARMYs, including family and friends, all of whose lives have been changed by BTS and/or Jung, that I was able to write the first sentence of this essay and anchor it around the word *I*.

These conversations delved into the impact of BTS and Jung, the role of shadow, and more. In the following sections, I've included highlights from these conversations, which took place over several months in person, in video chats and emails, and on social media. Through these longer-form excerpts, I wanted as much as possible to convey the participants' thoughts in a way that preserved the authenticity of their perspectives and their voices. This intention, too, is informed by my time working on VOW books and related narrative projects. Reading a VOW

narrative often feels like experiencing the narrator's journey with them. Similarly, my hope for including my interactions with these members of BTS and Jungian communities is that you, the reader, can journey more fully alongside me, and also witness the lively wisdom of these perspectives in their original forms.

ON THE POWER OF THE SHADOW WITH IPEK BURNETT

There's a common refrain in the BTS fandom: "You don't find BTS. BTS finds you when you need them the most." I've heard people talk about Jung that way, too, and I wonder if this is because both Jung and BTS resonate with people and artists interested in exploring, and acknowledging, their shadow selves. One of the first people I think of is my friend Ipek Burnett, a novelist and writer who explores social, cultural, and political issues through the lens of depth psychology. Her most recent book is *A Jungian Inquiry into the American Psyche: The Violence of Innocence*. Over tea, we chat about how her interest in psychology and creativity led her to Jung, and about the role of the unconscious and the imagination in art, life, and politics. On the latter subject, I like how she describes the role of shadow with such clarity:

> [Shadow] doesn't have to be evil, it doesn't have to be dark, but [rather] things that we don't own in ourselves and project onto others. And for Jung and Jungian psychology, it's a moral responsibility to understand and own our wholeness. Psychological

Kurt Cobain

insights can be very useful when we think about social, cultural, and political realities. Our narratives are so much about pride and power and victory. But in our shadow are all the repressions and oppressions, violent histories—the projection [of these shadows] between nations leads to wars. It can really help us reflect on political struggles, cultural polarization, and war.

ON THE POWER OF INTROSPECTION WITH YASSIN ADAM

Although Ipek isn't a BTS fan (she admits she doesn't know much about them beyond what I've mentioned to her), her comments make me think about how BTS's artistic (and commercial and cultural) power is uniquely derived in part from their ability to engage honestly with their shadows, and how crucial this is to their ability to embody this message authentically for their fans. This is also true for BTS fan Yassin Adam, an American actor of Somali descent based in Georgia. I first become aware of Yassin when one of his Twitter posts appears in my feed, in which he shares his admiration for BTS's *Map of the Soul* era and the Jungian concepts it explores. In his other posts, I appreciate the succinct, thoughtful candor with which he writes about his hopes and struggles in his journey as an actor. I first reach out to Yassin on Twitter, asking if he'd like to share some thoughts for this piece, and we continue our conversation over email. He writes:

A few months prior to the release of their EP *Map of the Soul:*

Persona, I was taking a psychology course and had learned a bit about Carl Jung's analytical psychology. BTS had me revisit the lessons I learned previously in a deeper way. I loved to try and predict the themes of upcoming BTS albums and/or concepts, and release dates. In order to do so this time around, I had to do some research on Carl Jung's works. I ended up also making friends in the fandom who studied or researched in that field as well. The *Map of the Soul* series came after the *Love Yourself* series of BTS albums. *Map of the Soul* expanded upon previous BTS themes by going deeper and exploring Jungian concepts of our personalities: the persona, shadow, and ego. My takeaway [from] this artistic progression was that in order to truly love yourself, you need a better understanding of who you are. BTS's engagement with Jungian ideas allowed me to take a more introspective look into myself. I was going through a lot of personal struggles at the time of *Map of the Soul*'s release. The band's taking me on this musical journey with them, exploring the self, allowed me to be able to relate to them on a more personal level. I related to them when they expressed their fears, and also when they expressed their aspirations. BTS didn't let their fears stop them from creating. They were able to connect to fans on this level, even at the height they were at in this point [in] their careers.

ON BTS AS "TOTAL ART" WITH MURRAY STEIN

These same ideas have been deeply explored by psychoanalyst Murray Stein, author of *Jung's Map of the Soul*, the book that BTS cites as the inspiration for the naming of their *Map of the Soul* series. When I send him an email requesting an interview, it is without much hope of a reply; I imagine he is inundated with requests from BTS fans since the surge in popularity of his book, and busy enough outside that with his teaching, analytical practice, and writing. To my surprise, I receive a warm reply the next day, asking if it's all right if we correspond over email, given the time difference (he is based in Zürich). In his written response to my questions, Murray tells me that initially he was unaware that his book was being discussed as an influence on BTS. He had no idea that the surge in interest was thanks to BTS's *Map of the Soul: Persona* EP and *Map of the Soul: 7* album. He writes:

One day Dr. Shin-Ichiro Otsuka, a student at the International School of Analytical Psychology in Zurich, where I teach, came up to me and asked me if I was aware that my book was listed on the BTS website as recommended reading. I asked him, "What's BTS?" I had not heard of the group and am not a follower of pop-music artists. That was my introduction to BTS. The next thing I heard, again from Dr. Otsuka, was that BTS was going to use the title of my book in their new album and would be including in their lyrics references

A Beginner's Guide to

UNDERSTANDING K-POP GENERATIONS

FIRST GENERATION—Korea's bestselling album of 1998: Seo Taiji, Seo Tai Ji

In the 1980s, Korean dancers grooved with Black American GIs in the underground clubs of Itaewon, near the US military base in Seoul, South Korea. One of them, Hyun Jin-young, crafted a Korean hip-hop style that drew heavily on new jack swing in songs like "Sad Mannequin" (1990) and "You in Vague Memory" (1992). His labelmates Seo Taiji and Boys took the combination further with hits like "Come Back Home" (1995). They spoke directly to the concerns of young South Koreans, soundtracking their dance moves with pensive lyrics: "My life is blocked by the fear of tomorrow."

Next came the boy group H.O.T., who combined aggression with tenderness. On "Descent of Warriors" (1996), they railed against violence and presented themselves as defenders of youth; megahit "Candy" (1996) was a classic,

peppy boy-band song with a vibrant music video to match. Baby V.O.x, a girl group, experimented with self-presentation, appearing as comic book fighters in "To Men" (1997), bohemians in "Why" (2000), and hip-hop dancers in "Xcstasy" (2004).

Their ambition was striking: they told authentic stories of youth, incorporating an arresting visual language that reflected a globalizing culture. It could weigh heavily on the human beings carrying it. **Park Ji-yoon** gained fame with "Coming of Age Ceremony" (2000), in which a young woman straightforwardly seduced a lover. Idols often re-create the sexy music video when they turn twenty. Korea's legal age of consent. But Park, who

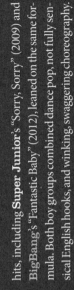

SEO TAIJI

was only eighteen at the time, has spoken about how emotionally unequipped she was for the song and her resulting notoriety.

SECOND GENERATION—Artists on the Billboard Hot 100: Wonder Girls, CL, PSY

In the 2000s, South Korea transitioned from the Asian financial crisis to a period of rapid economic growth and social change. K-pop's second generation defined itself by projecting confidence amid ongoing uncertainty.

Girls' Generation debuted with a message that was blunt but kind. On "Into the New World" (2007) they sang, "Don't wait for any miracle. Our rough path in front of us might be a challenge, but we can't give up." It became an enduring song of solidarity for women and LGBTQ+ groups, later appearing in the Hong Kong pro-democracy protests.

With "I Am the Best" (2011), 2NE1 exemplified an era of songs that were flamboyant, catchy, and almost absurdly cocky. In the campy music video, the girl group danced in studded leather outfits, chanting like a militia. They were also in on the joke, fighting to get out of straitjackets and using custom baseball bats to smash records—physical records, not the chart and sales records most K-pop stars try to break. Other

WONDER GIRLS

hits, including **Super Junior**'s "Sorry, Sorry" (2009) and BigBang's "Fantastic Baby" (2012), leaned on the same formula. Both boy groups combined dance pop, not fully sensical English hooks, and winking, swaggering choreography. The genre's eclectic influences could also meld into something idiosyncratic and fun, as **Infinite** demonstrated on "The Chaser" (2012). The song used electronic beats, rock guitars, orchestral strings, and brass alongside demanding changes to the tempo and key. Through the boy group's visible effort and skill, it felt not only coherent but propulsive.

For many global fans, K-pop's unpredictable mix of confidence, silliness, and finesse was its appeal. As Korean content spread on YouTube, it became increasingly popular within Korean American and other immigrant groups. The performers showed possibilities for being Asian beyond the limited stereotypes in Western media.

THIRD GENERATION—First K-pop idol group to perform at Coachella: Blackpink

As labels matured and fans gave real-time feedback, the third generation of idols invested more in their artistry. It was thrilling to watch **Seventeen**—a boy group that handled their own songwriting and production—refine their identity in real time, shifting from the rowdy "Mansae" (2015) and the zany "Very Nice" (2016) to the intricate choreography and storytelling of "Don't Wanna Cry" (2017).

Several of this era's successful artists had at least one quality antithetical to prior K-pop rules. This conceptual instability was part of their appeal. Mamamoo pushed against K-beauty standards and the expectation that each member should have a single persona within the group. Instead, "Décalcomanie" (2016) and "Wind Flower" (2018) showcased

how their myriad personalities merged to form complex narratives.

Around this time, it became difficult to define K-pop as a genre or an industry. The Rose, an indie band that didn't emphasize dance or visual appeal, won over mainstream audiences with "Sorry" (2017). Holland's "Neverland" (2018) was the first debut from an openly gay idol. BTS found unprecedented success by trying everything from hip-hop to art pop. The possibilities were by no means endless, and performers who deviated from norms were viciously criticized. Still, by the close of this generation, there was an emerging disconnect between what major labels offered and what fans chose to engage with.

BLACKPINK

FOURTH GENERATION—Single-album sales of over two million copies: Stray Kids, TXT, aespa

In the fourth generation, production teams have a full toolbox and regularly use it. NewJeans is holding the Korean charts in a chokehold by doing everything, all at once. The girl group's outfits copy millennial styles, their music swings from low-fi R&B to Baltimore club beats, and music videos like "Cool with You" (2023) tell intricate stories about love, perception, and possession. The highly anticipated girl group aespa debuted with "Black Mamba" (2022), set in a fully realized metaverse.

The scene is rife with melancholy and a longing for weirdness. BIBI's "BAD SAD AND MAD" (2021) draws uncomfortable parallels between BDSM and a

bad relationship, while stretching the singer's voice from a murmur to a scream. In the video for "0X1 = LOVESONG (I Know I Love You)" (2021), TOMORROW X TOGETHER scream rock vocals while traversing a crumbling landscape, channeling the angst of leaving boyhood. Stray Kids' body of work, particularly the *Oddinary* EP (2022), explores the selves that lurk beneath our most polished facades—and what might happen if they got out.

The fourth generation seems to be maxing out on both emotion and musical styles. Is this a symptom of our content-saturated time, or a creative renaissance?

TOMORROW X TOGETHER

W hat's commonly known as K-pop spans the 1990s to the present, and is divided into four generations. The first generation established the idol group structure, in which boy groups and girl groups perform a mixture of pop and rap with synchronized choreography and heavy fan interaction. Second-generation idols refined the concept and, thanks to YouTube's rise in 2006, made Korean music go global. The third generation reigned during the 2010s, exploring K-pop's boundaries while dramatically raising its commercial ceiling. And for the last several years, fourth-generation idols have been making generic, uninteresting noise or completely changing the game, depending on whom you ask.

—Aku Ammah-Tagoe

to the Jungian concept of the "persona." This really surprised me. I was not sure how this concept would come across in their performances. But when I finally saw BTS's performances online, I found them absolutely thrilling and fascinating. This is beyond music! It's akin to opera, or what Richard Wagner called "total art"—music, theater, dance, lighting effects. A BTS performance is what we call, in the Jungian world, "numinous," or what the scholar of religion Rudolf Otto termed "Mysterium tremendum et fascinans" ("a mystery tremendous and fascinating"). BTS's performances and albums have that effect on their fans. It's a type of religious experience. What convinced me that they were serious about using psychology to bring more consciousness to the world was their [2018] appearance at the United Nations and listening to the talk of RM. This really impressed me, and so I was delighted that BTS would be using their enormous popularity in the world to communicate an important psychological message to their millions of fans.

Murray has responded to the increased interest in his book, and in Jungian psychology more broadly, by participating in interviews and projects for ARMY-run sites and podcasts, including *Speaking of Jung* (a website and podcast that explores the psychology of Jung through discussions with Jungian analysts) and *The Rhizomatic Revolution Review* (an online, open-access, peer-reviewed journal focused on the art, fandom, economic effects, and socio-cultural forces generated by BTS and ARMY).

What strikes me while listening to his various interviews, and in our correspondence, is his sincere appreciation for BTS as both artists and human beings, and his efforts to make Jungian concepts as accessible as possible to people encountering them for the first time. Concerned that his book might be difficult to understand for younger BTS fans unfamiliar with Jungian psychology, he wrote the book *Map of the Soul—7: Persona, Shadow, and Ego in the World of BTS*, in which he offers an extremely accessible introduction to the fundamentals of Jungian psychology, accompanied by an examination of the album *Map of the Soul: 7* that brings to light the layers of meaning within the songs—a kind of legend for the album for those interested in engaging with it through a Jungian lens. I can't help but wonder what this book would have meant to me as a young art student beginning to grapple with questions of identity and wholeness—perhaps I wouldn't have given up on Jung so easily back then if I'd had access to it. Murray sees BTS's lyrics as:

> genuine teachings about how the psyche functions [that] have had a strong educational impact on millions of people who would otherwise never have been exposed to these important insights. What BTS has done with the concepts is to give them a very personal expression,

speaking about how they have incorporated them into their own consciousness and how they have helped them deal with their individual life issues. Their enormous success has created the problem all celebrities face, which is to stay conscious that they are not the image that people have of them—they are who they are. If they get too caught up in their famous personas, they lose contact with themselves, and this can have tragic consequences, as we often see in the short and unhappy lives of the famous. BTS have used themselves to illustrate the meaning of Jung's psychological concepts.

In his book *Map of the Soul—7*, Murray writes:

> They strike me as a serious, thoughtful group of young people raising consciousness… increasing self-acceptance, and fighting the plague of suicide that besets so many parts of the world today, especially among young people. They are saying that life is worth living. I support this with all my heart. And maybe [BTS's] *Map of the Soul* will support these efforts, too.

ON FOLLOWING THE ENERGY WITH MELISSA WERNER

Melissa Werner, an Alabama-based Jungian analyst, echoes these assertions. She describes "Interlude: Shadow" (SUGA's solo track on *Map of the Soul: 7*, in which he sings and raps about his greed, ambition, and lust for power) as "maybe the best explanation of shadow that I have ever seen."

I first learn about Melissa through listening to an interview on the *Speaking of Jung* podcast, in which she and host Laura London talk about their experience of seeing BTS in concert during the pandemic. I'm fascinated by Melissa's perspective as a seventy-one-year-old Jungian ARMY who came to both Jung and BTS later in life. Melissa became a Jungian analyst just five years ago and a fan of BTS three years ago; she talks about both in terms of joyful discovery, and how they have enriched her life profoundly. When we speak over a video call, I'm immediately taken by her bright energy and humor. She tells me:

> I was a college professor in my forties when I went to a Jungian analyst and she said, "You need to pay attention to your dreams and record your dreams." That was the beginning of an analysis that lasted more than twenty years. I had no idea I would become an analyst. Jung, in my personal analytic work, probably changed my life and saved my soul. It gave me a life that's richer and fuller and in more abundance than I would've ever found without Jung.
>
> I started listening to BTS in 2020. I would listen to their music and I would cry. I even went back to my own analyst, who's in her nineties now, and said, "What is wrong with me? I'm a grandmother!" I said, "What is going on? I am so moved by this music and these men. Am I

missing something and there's a real deficit going on in me and I need to address that within?" I could not figure it out, because it's like this love affair but not with these individuals. It's love here with this group, this situation, this worldview that came out of left field for me, came out of the underground, and it also gave me life. My analyst just reminded me that we are called to go where our energy is. And that's where my energy is.

Of their broader cultural impact, Melissa says:

> I don't think of them as the largest K-pop band in the world. They're the largest band in the world as far as I'm concerned, so it's like they are a cultural movement. This, to me, is something so huge from the underground, from the chthonic place. I don't think people realize this cultural shift is going on, this shift that's centered out of this very small country that, for me, is surrounded by this music and this whole idea of loving yourself. The first thing you've got to take care of is yourself and your relationship to yourself, which is what we all are about as Jungians. It's a movement. BTS, and the country of South Korea, seem to be capturing something about the future within the zeitgeist of the world. I'm curious. That is a future I'm interested in. It's how Dionysus crept in. He crept in from the underground.

ON THE DUALITY OF ETERNAL YOUTH AND MATURITY WITH JEEYOUN KIM

When I tell Melissa I'd love to hear from a Korean Jungian ARMY, she suggests that I speak to Dr. Jeeyoun Kim, a psychotherapist from Seoul. Jeeyoun has a unique perspective that encompasses multiple positionalities—as a Jungian analyst, as a Korean, and as a BTS fan. I'm interested in how and why she was drawn to Jung and BTS, and in learning from her about the broader influence of BTS in Korean society. Calling from Geneva, where she is now based, Jeeyoun describes her own introduction to Jung as deeply rooted in her country's political history:

> In my personal history, in my country, I was born and raised under the dictatorship. It triggered in me many questions about the nature of life—in Jungian terminology, it's the "shadow of the self." Who am I, what is the purpose of life, why can't we live peacefully with our neighbors?
>
> This ego and self, the ego's journey to search for the self, the bigger entity, is all about this journey. We call it a "night sea journey." So it's a dark night and people try to find out the answer and they go through this, in the situation of hopelessness. But sometimes you have courage to keep hope. This is what I found in all the great writers' books and in Jung's books, and also in the songs of BTS.

When Jeeyoun talks about her initial impression of BTS, she says she felt the Jungian resonance immediately:

I was caught by the song "Fake Love." It was their first performance in the United States. The song was really catchy and they looked extremely beautiful. Also, I was very impressed by their almost perfect dance.

Around that time, I was interested in a certain topic of Jungian psychology. I was giving a lecture about the so-called puer and the problem of eternal youth. I have some artistic clients. They have a specific psychology, which I used to have too—it was one of my issues when I was younger. In our psychology, there are two aspects. One is puer. The other is senex. Puer is eternal youth; you are creative, you are youthful, you are fun-loving. We can see these characteristics in BTS. At the same time, senex is the opposite, but this is what we need. It's about self-discipline, humility and maturity and reliability.

In ancient Korean history, there was a dynasty called Shilla. There were Hwarang—young male aristocrat warriors. Kim Taehyung [BTS member V] played this role in the TV series *Hwarang: The Poet Warrior Youth*. The Hwarang had to be excellent in academics, martial arts, and art, especially song and dance. And they wore makeup and accessories, earrings. In those days of the Goryeo dynasty and Shilla dynasty, the aristocrat males enjoyed this

kind of beauty. Aesthetics were very important. It was almost part of the ethics. So there might be a combination or connection between puer and senex.

Then when I saw BTS's performance, I thought, They're personified puer and senex, an almost ideal combination of these virtues, because to reach their level of perfection in dance, they are not geniuses—they've practiced. I was very moved when I looked at their history, how long they had to endure [their training], and how devoted they were as very young men. This virtue is very rare. You don't find it everywhere. But as young men, they endured this and they had very strong self-discipline. At the same time, they are fun-loving and a little foolish sometimes. And they're very creative. So this duality looks very contrasted, but they have it all.

When I look at their songs and their lyrics, I find my younger self in them. When you really listen to their songs, the suffering they had to go through is who I really am. These all are sufferings to find out who you are and the journey to listen to the inner voice. I really like the song "Epiphany." I share this song with many of my clients. This is our basic agony, the lack of self-love.

When I ask her to talk about the broader significance of BTS in Korean society, she talks about their song "Spring Day" as something that created a sense of community following the *Sewol* ferry disaster:

In Korean we called the song a "tear button" ["눈물버튼" in Korean, "nunmul beoteun" romanized] because it reflects this collective trauma. So most Koreans know it and what it means. People feel grateful to BTS. They don't just sing something pink or sweet. That's why we feel that all their songs are very authentic, and that they're genuine. It's always like they express themself as members of society who live in the same era as everyone else—of course, not only in Korea. We are all connected. The big, big Eros. I think they gave this sense of Eros to Korean society.

When I hear her mention "Eros," I am struck by the frequent mentions of love in various forms—self-love, desire for connection and wholeness—in my conversations so far about BTS and Jung. And I think of how the various expressions of love for a group like BTS and what they represent are not simply forms of tribute but often result in the simultaneous expansion of one's worldview and inner life. My friend Aku Ammah-Tagoe, the author of the brief K-pop primer that accompanies this piece, is an exemplar of this idea.

ON EXPANSIVE ENGAGEMENT AND CONCERT-GOING WITH AKU AMMAH-TAGOE

Aku is an Oakland, California–based educator and writer. She and I have known each other since 2018, and I think she would agree that while our friendship predates and transcends our appreciation of BTS, it has grown richer through this shared connection. In the summer of 2020, when I was just a few months into my BTS rabbit hole but already deeply invested, I had a hunch she might also like them. It wasn't just because I knew she liked pop music, or that I thought she was open-minded enough to listen to and appreciate pop music in a language she didn't know. It was because I thought she might enjoy the layers of meaning within the songs and music videos, and the layers of meaningful experience that being a fan entails. So one day, while I was out on a run, I stopped by her apartment in the Mission District of San Francisco.

"We started talking and the subject of pop music came up," recalls Aku when we meet over tea, "and you were like, 'Oh, you mentioned boy bands. Do you know BTS?' And I said, 'No, not really.' And so you very generously made me a playlist."

Later, as we went for walks during shelter-in-place and as her interest in BTS grew, the band gradually took up more and more space in our conversations. By the following year, Aku was deeply immersed. Aku is the kind of person who, when she finds something she loves, takes the time and effort to learn about the context in which it has come to exist, to more fully understand and appreciate it—an embodiment of the motto "The more you put in, the more you get out." In the case of BTS, she took an expansive, engaged interest in the history of K-pop and became a fan of other K-pop artists. She also started taking Korean-language lessons. More recently, she has been developing a podcast with the first season dedicated to K-pop. This kind of thoughtful investment and dedication is very Aku, and also reflective of many BTS fans.

"When I discovered BTS, I was a couple of years out of a PhD program," she says, "and I found entering the world of ARMY just as intellectually stimulating, and sometimes more so, because people were talking about so many different kinds of things with so much depth. Most people who enter the BTS fandom in a serious way start thinking about, OK, what are the structures and systems in place to (1) produce pop music, (2) circulate it around the world, (3) talk about it and critique it, assign it cultural value? And then, (4), ask: How do other people respond to me and my interest in pop music and how is that meaningful?"

In terms of BTS's exploration and embodiment of Jungian concepts, she claims to have only a passing knowledge of Jungian psychology, but she feels a strong affinity with its core ideas around wholeness. She says:

> I would say it was something I was very attuned to already, and specifically my version of it was various forms of attention—being able to know yourself, see yourself, see what is really there, and be able to talk about it and describe it. It's really empowering. So rather than trying to cut off or eliminate bad parts of yourself, being able to really understand who you are.
>
> What I really love about *Map of the Soul*, and a lot of BTS's music, is that you are looking at different parts of yourself, you are describing them, but then you're also doing things that allow

you to engage more fully with yourself. And this is where I think the dance-and-movement aspect of what they do is so important, and the style and visual aspects of what they do are so important. And even the act of singing, because I think all those can be ways of engaging with yourself. I think it's a way of learning more. I feel like there was a gap between what I knew intellectually and what I knew in a really embodied way that I was actually able to put into practice in my life. And I think BTS, by presenting a rich embodiment of their own messages, is able to bridge that gap between what you know and what you are able to do.

> I love the song "Inner Child." It just has such a pure sweetness, and it's something that I know a lot of my high school students, for example, would be like, *Oh, that's so cringe. It's not cool. I'm so embarrassed for that guy. Why is he singing to his inner child?* But I actually think the refrain, "We're gonna change, we're gonna change"—just the act of saying that over and over and over, that kind of thing—is meditative, it's a mantra. It's deeply reassuring. The whole work of that song is imagining your inner child, talking to your inner child, and then trying to bring your inner child with you into the present, which is what many therapists would also tell you to do.

Early in Aku's BTS journey, I invited her to join a group chat with me and my friend Shan, the first ARMY pal I'd made and whom I thought of as my Bangtan Yoda. Based in DC, Shan is a journalist and an editor at *The Atlantic*. She has been my early guide and fellow explorer through the world of BTS, often texting me updates, funny ARMY-made memes, and insightful observations on production, song arrangement, and the K-pop industry. Shan, Aku, and I texted prolifically— at a certain point I realized I was in touch with them more frequently than with my own family. At a time when the pandemic restricted our ability to safely travel and gather in person, this felt like a lifeline, a way to transcend survival mode and connect with joy.

During this time, the prospect of us ever getting to see BTS perform live felt like nothing more than a dim hope. The pandemic had forced the cancellation of their world tour for *Map of the Soul: 7*. Even if they did hold concerts in the future, we knew the general difficulty of securing tickets (the intense scramble for past tour tickets has been variously described by ARMYs as "a bloodbath" and "the Hunger Games"). There was also uncertainty around the members' mandatory military service enlistment.

Then, in September 2021, as the Delta variant waned (and before Omicron was identified), BTS announced they would be hosting four concerts at SoFi Stadium in LA in November and December. Demand was predictably high. Hope was still dim. But miraculously, we secured tickets for two of the concert nights.

Seeing BTS live was a euphoric, emotional, and thrilling experience— due as much to their performance as to the energy of the sixty thousand other ARMYs in attendance. Watching footage of past BTS tours, I had known that their concerts are filled with a twinkling sea of fan light sticks (known as ARMY bombs). But being part of this sea in person brought an overwhelming feeling of communion.

Afterward, having danced and sung and screamed for over two hours, I was a bundle of sweaty exhaustion and restless elation. It was a feeling that brought me back to the avid, indie-gig-going of my younger days in London: leaving a venue at the end of a concert among throngs of other fans and heading to the nearest Tube station together, then piling onto a train carriage and drawing curious looks from the locals. The difference then was that the bond was mostly unspoken— it wasn't cool to acknowledge that we'd just been to the same concert or that you admired the verticality of someone's Robert Smith–esque back-combed hairdo. But at the BTS concert, both before and after the show, fans would openly call out compliments on a stranger's outfit, especially if it was humorous and/or clear that the person had spent a lot of time and effort making it. Strangers placed freebies in my hands, mostly personalized pouches containing candy, friendship bracelets, sanitary wipes, and BTS photo cards. (As much as I am not a merchandise-buying ARMY, I am physically incapable of throwing away anything BTS-related that someone has gifted me.) The post-concert atmosphere felt less like the aftermath of a show and more like the next stage of a festival, as fans continued to mingle, buy snacks and merch, and catch up.

ON BTS AS A MEANS OF CONNECTION, WITH CANDACE EPPS-ROBERTSON AND PHOENIX EPPS-ROBERTSON

It was in this environment that I met ARMYs in person whom I'd known of and admired only in the online ARMYverse. Among these were Candace Epps-Robertson, an English professor based in North Carolina, and her daughter Phoenix, a high school student. Candace found her way to BTS through her daughter, and over the past few years it has been delightful to read, through Candace's tweets and her blog, about how their relationship has been positively affected by their shared connection to BTS. Candace tells me:

> Phoenix asked me if I knew BTS. I said no and thought that would be the end, but it wasn't. She filled our home with their music and changed our lives. I was in awe of her dedication to learning Korean, inspired by how she took every opportunity she could to teach us about BTS, and I loved her happiness. It was one of those situations where you are happy because the other person is happy, but at some point, that changed for me, and BTS became a source of joy and inspiration for me too.

Phoenix adds:

> I decided to share my interest in BTS with my mom because it felt like something that was becoming really important to me. I had started to feel the positive impact the music was having on me, and

I hoped it would have a similar effect on her. It's given us lots of life-changing opportunities and a new thing to bond over.

Candace talks about BTS's impact in terms of joy and authenticity:

Their music and philosophy are a great reminder of what's possible when people work together to bring joy and respite through art. Because of this attention to joy, they've encouraged me to be a better parent, educator, and all-around human. I don't mean to suggest that their focus is only on feeling good—it's not toxic positivity, but their ability to bring to their fans a kind of authenticity that acknowledges that life is hard. However, we can still find joy and deserve happiness, even amid chaos.

When I ask her about the Jungian connection, she says:

Honestly, I'd not thought much about Jung before BTS. In grad school, I read *Man and His Symbols* and later read selections from Dr. Murray Stein's *Jung's Map of the Soul*. I would never have guessed my musical interests would have brought me back to Jung, but they did. I was most interested in how BTS's use of Jung connects to themes around identity, growth, and the challenges of learning (and unlearning) who you are in relation to the world around you. I think about this quite a bit as it relates to being middle-aged, because this is another one of those moments when life's transitions almost force us to confront the roles and patterns we've learned and ask questions about who and what we are. That it is indeed a journey to discover (or sometimes recover) who you are is a lesson I carry with me. It's not easy to do at any age, but their music expresses this desire quite clearly.

ON BTS PULLING YOU THROUGH HARD TIMES WITH CHAN HOI KEI

When I visit Hong Kong in spring 2023, I meet up with my cousin Chan Hoi Kei (Kei Kei to friends and family), a fashion designer and long-time K-pop fan. I believe my first awareness of K-pop came from her—years ago I'd seen her Facebook posts about the group Big Bang, and I recall that in the summer of 2019, when she and her friend came to London and stayed with my parents, I asked her what her plans were for the trip and she replied, "We're going to see BTS at Wembley Arena." Having only a vague awareness of them at the time, I had said with a shrug, "OK, have fun." (I've lost count of the number of times I've wished I could have gone back to that summer and asked to go along with her. There might have been a chance to get a last-minute ticket; I could have been part of a concert that has gone down as legend in the fandom: it was BTS's first time performing at this iconic venue, and it was at this concert that, during the encore, ARMYs surprised and moved BTS by serenading them with the chorus of "Young Forever." I wish all this, until my wiser self shows up to remind me that it's OK; I found them at just the right time.)

Since becoming a BTS fan, I have been in more regular contact with Kei Kei. In the past few years, our texts have started with BTS and ended with well wishes, and sometimes along the way we talk about the political situation in Hong Kong, and the psychological and economic impacts of severe COVID-19 restrictions that initially saw closed borders, followed by twenty-one-day hotel quarantine requirements for inbound travelers. (The government finally lifted its quarantine restrictions in September of 2022.)

My trip back to Hong Kong is my first since 2018. I notice the different kinds of quiet that now permeate daily life; many Hong Kongers have left in recent years, and most of those who've remained watch what they say in public. In June 2020, Beijing imposed a national security law on Hong Kong following a year of pro-democracy protests and unrest. The legislation criminalizes virtually all forms of dissent and gives police sweeping new powers. In recent years, activists have been imprisoned, journalists have been forced into exile, and teachers have been fired for mentioning the Tiananmen massacre to their students. The city feels both intimately familiar and deeply, irrevocably changed from the political turmoil of the past few years.

I meet Kei Kei at a restaurant in Mongkok, where, without having consulted the other, we both have turned up in different BTS T-shirts. Afterward, we squeeze our way through the dense crowds in search of a tong sui stall to satisfy our dessert cravings, and on the way I point at a giant billboard advertising what seems to be a K-pop boy band. I ask her who they are, and she replies,

"Oh, that's Mirror. They're a Hong Kong boy band. They got really popular during the pandemic."

She tells me that Mirror was formed in 2018 and have helped infuse the city with a much-needed sense of joy and escapism, as well as hometown pride. Their popularity appears to transcend demographics. The deep social divisions arising from these past few years—mainly between "yellow" (pro-democracy) and "blue" (pro–police and government) affiliations—have manifested in a multitude of ways, from ideologically opposed family members refusing to sit down to eat dinner together, to the boycotting of businesses whose allegiances do not align with those of their customers. So it doesn't surprise me when Kei Kei says that pro-democracy Hong Kongers embraced the group only once they were satisfied that they "supported Hong Kong and not Beijing." Although Mirror has avoided explicit political declarations, the group's songs have been adopted by some members of the pro-democracy movement as anthems of perseverance, and the group has come under fire online from mainland China social media users accusing the group of supporting Hong Kong's independence and promoting homosexuality. (Later, when I look up their videos, the influence of K-pop—and BTS in particular—is evident, from their choreography to their cheerful sincerity and even their logo.)

Kei Kei has been a fan of BTS since 2016 and cites their debut performance of "Blood Sweat and Tears" as her rabbit-hole moment. She was initially struck by their powerful performance, before being charmed by their goofiness in YouTube clips and on their variety show *Run BTS*. She credits BTS's popularity in Hong Kong with what locals call their 貼地 (romanized: "tip dei," Cantonese slang for "down-to-earth") attitude, as much as their talent. Kei Kei tells me:

> Hong Kongers see BTS as more affable and down-to-earth than other K-pop artists. They communicate a lot more with their fans. With the previous generation of K-pop artists like Big Bang, social media wasn't as prevalent, and we just accepted a certain distance from them—they're stars, they're meant to be cool and aloof. And back then, they might not release new music for a long time, so you might not hear from them for a while. Actually, even today, with some artists there might be two years before a mini album comes out. And a lot of artists don't go on social media and chat with fans as often as BTS does. It also feels like there's more communication between BTS fans online, and so there's more of an interactive, cohesive feeling within the fandom. Some artists might chat on social media at the beginning of their career, but after they get famous they tend to do that a lot less.

When we get back to my hotel room, we eat tong yuen while appreciating the evening cityscape and chatting more about BTS and Jung. Kei Kei describes how BTS opened up her interest in psychology:

When the album came out, I bought the book *Map of the Soul—7*. It was actually hard to find, because so many fans wanted to know the inspiration behind the album. I thought the songs explored the themes and concepts in the book really well. BTS had previously touched on psychology, through the song "Magic Shop," but it was more fully realized in *Map of the Soul: 7*. The song "ON" came out just before the pandemic, but it seemed to have a rebellious, warrior-like feeling about it that matched the spirit of a lot of Hong Kong people at the time. It was the beginning of COVID and lockdown, and "ON" had this *keep going, don't give up* energy to it, while "Black Swan" connected with the darker side, with feeling down. That song is about losing passion for something you've devoted yourself to and also about losing your sense of self in that passion. It made me reflect on where I was in my career as a designer, made me question my success and my path: Is this still what I want to do?

I've never been much of a reader—I'm not cultivated! If I hadn't got into psychology through BTS, I probably wouldn't have read a lot of other psychology books. Even if I couldn't remember all the lessons at the time, it all added up. It helped me deal with depression after quitting a job because of a toxic boss. It helped me own my emotions. I felt like my EQ level increased.

Toward the end of the evening, Kei Kei shows me the small photo album she's brought along containing BTS photocards and stickers. As we look over these together, it feels a little like we're teenagers again, or kids sharing Pokémon cards. Of course we never used to hang out like this, given our age difference (I'm over a decade older) and the fact that we grew up on opposite sides of the world. But child me, growing up in a small English town without anyone to nerd out with over Cantopop—I know she would have really loved that.

I've taken away so much from all these conversations and felt many moments of illumination and connection that continue to reverberate months later. Kei Kei and Yassin talking about "Black Swan"'s exploration of the relationship between self, art, and passion—and Ipek's and Melissa's thoughts on the nature of shadow—echo my own contemplations. It has been only in the last few years that I've been able to articulate the power of shadow in my fiction writing, which is concerned largely with the histories Chinese women and girls inherit and what we do with them, and with longing, belonging, and connection in various forms. It is no coincidence that the stories that have felt the most scary, challenging, and thrilling to write—the ones that confront and explore shadow longings and fears—are the ones that have resonated most strongly with readers. Writers sometimes talk about the point at which they stop writing their characters and the characters start writing themselves. It can sound like some kind of mysterious writer-magic BS, but it isn't really; it's more about being tuned in to the deepest wants and fears of your character and acknowledging, then listening to, the unconscious parts of yourself that manifested this person in the first

Being able to give frank, public expression to something that once felt so impossibly raw and shrouded in shame and silence feels like not just a sign of healing but also a means to it.

place. Yes, writers constantly draw inspiration from the world around them, but inspiration invariably takes root because it speaks to something deep inside you. I know writers who listen to certain songs, or entire playlists, to access a character, or describe the process as "getting into character," like an actor does. I know of others who meditate so they can come to their desk with a more spacious, attentive mind, or take breaks to go on a brisk walk or run, or to do the dishes (anything mindless and repetitive to rest the brain but also allow the unconscious to slip through). I try to do some combination of the above, depending on the circumstances.

Meanwhile, what is usually described as writer's block has tended to occur when I'm not tuned in to my mind and body—when I've taken a pause in journaling or when I've fallen out of my exercise routine and into procrastination, often a response to stress or fatigue. It's no wonder that, during these periods when I'm closed off and lethargic, the creativity does not flow. When Aku described how BTS has helped her close the gap between intellectual knowledge and embodied wisdom and doing, it made me think of these "blocked" situations, and how BTS's music provokes a visceral response in me—depending on the song, it can elicit an outpouring of tears or of joy, or an unshakable urge to dance or run. The effect is so immediate that it enables me to override my tendencies toward the overly cerebral and abstract. In this way, the combined effect of the messages in their music—how they embody them as individuals and collectively, and the physical response their music engenders—has helped me close the gaps between knowing, doing, and feeling, and move toward *embodying*.

The conversations for this piece have also made me think about how I previously tried to limit the expression of my shadow to my fiction, somewhat unsuccessfully. It was only after my first book of stories, *Last of Her Name*, was published that I realized my fiction wasn't only a container for expressing and exploring shadow impulses (and, I'll admit, an excuse to hide behind my characters), but also, once it was out in the world, a way to spark conversation and connection around taboo subjects. Talking about my characters forced me to step out from behind them, a rather uncomfortable but ultimately helpful sensation. And these recent conversations have no

doubt led me to ways I might step out even further from my comfort zone, shadow not just in tow but leading the way. Writing this piece is one example of that. Another is speaking in March 2023 at an event commemorating the two-year anniversary of the Atlanta spa shootings, part of a live streamed, multicity rally that included Atlanta, New York, Denver, San Francisco, and Detroit. Being able to give frank, public expression to something that once felt so impossibly raw and shrouded in shame and silence feels like not just a sign of healing but also a means to it.

Candace's emphasis on midlife as an almost unavoidable time to "confront the roles and patterns we've learned and ask questions about who and what we are" reflects my own deeper questioning, in the wake of the pandemic and the Atlanta shootings, of what I needed to unlearn and relearn, in order to be whole. Thinking about Melissa's embrace of a significant career and life change in her sixties, and her continued commitment to joyful discovery in her seventies, fills me with admiration, and a more expansive curiosity about what awaits me in my later decades, if I'm lucky enough to meet them.

These conversations keep reminding me of how BTS, collectively and individually, embody and express the desire for self-knowledge and self-acceptance so clearly, and that this is work anyone can engage in at any time of life, whether they're a twentysomething global superstar, an octogenarian Jungian analyst, a high schooler, or a middle-aged writer. And I've become more conscious than before of the many other people out there who, whether or not their lives have been changed by BTS and Jung, are

nevertheless grappling with their own challenges around identity and growth and striving to know and love themselves. At times this awareness moves me to the point where I can't help but form a sentimental image of a vast, luminous sea, each dot of light twinkling with effort.

The period during which these conversations took place—between January and late April of 2023—coincided with my stepping out of my role as executive director of Voice of Witness. To leave an organization that I helped create and had dedicated myself to building over almost fifteen years, and that had been such a defining, fulfilling, and consuming part of my life, was not a step I took lightly. That I still loved and believed in the work, and held my colleagues in great affection and esteem, made it a difficult decision, and one I am still processing the aftermath of. But as sorrowful and frightening as it was to take that leap, the challenges and discoveries of the past few years have forced me to reexamine my priorities; it felt right for me to finally take some time for myself and see how and who else I can be.

I had made the decision just before I began working on this piece, and somewhat naively didn't foresee how fortunate I was to be accompanied by all these Jungian and ARMY voices through this fraught, uncertain time of transition—voices that, essentially, affirmed the rightness of questioning and seeking, and the necessity of closing one chapter in order to open a new one.

At the time of writing, it has been three months since my transition away from Voice of Witness. I've taken more time than ever before to rest, reflect, and spend time with loved ones near and far. I've been writing and reading more, while also resisting compulsive productivity (good antidotes being immersing myself in K-dramas, going on aimless drives, and staring at trees and clouds). I've severed relationships that I realized were causing me harm, and allowed new, healthier ones to flourish in their place, meeting new people and having rich conversations about life, art, death, food, AAPI storytelling, and everything in between, while also periodically retreating into hermit mode. And I've begun writing down my dreams, a practice also kept by Carl Jung.

Through all of the above, and through various other forms of doing and not doing, I suppose I have been trying to open up space and stillness in myself, and in that new space, letting different possibilities for the next phase of life take root without trying to control too much. Back in my young artist days, my attempts to engage with Jung and the exploration of wholeness felt like getting lost and frustrated in a darkened maze. This time around, the exploration is no less mysterious. But the maze feels less like a claustrophobic puzzle and more like a structure holding multiple openings and possibilities, and where hitting a dead end isn't the end of the world; it just means you turn yourself around and start walking in another direction.

BTS is currently on a break. They made the announcement to fans in June of 2022 on YouTube, on their ninth anniversary. Sitting around a dinner table in their once-shared apartment, RM, Jin, SUGA, j-hope, Jimin, V, and Jung Kook shared the news with frank and sometimes tearful honesty. With visible frustration, RM said:

I started music and became BTS because I had a message for the world. But at some point I haven't been sure what kind of group we are [anymore], and for me, it was a big deal that I didn't know... I've always thought BTS was different from other groups, but the problem with K-pop is that they don't give you time to mature. You have to keep producing music, to keep doing something. There's no time left for growth. I've changed as a human over the past ten years, so I needed to think and have some alone time. Right now when we're at our best I feel like I should be contributing something to the world, but I don't know what that is.

Jimin said the members were "slowly trying to figure things out now" and that "we're starting to think about what kind of artists we each want to be remembered as by our fans... we're trying to find our identity and that's an exhausting and long process."

SUGA clarified, "It's not that we're disbanding! We're just living apart for a while," and j-hope added, "I hope you see that it's a healthy plan. It's something we all need." Jung Kook revealed that *Map of the Soul: 7,* released two years prior, was intended to mark the end of the group's "first chapter." That record should have culminated in a lengthy world tour and opened up this next chapter of the members as individual artists. "This timing should have come to us earlier, but I guess we held it off. We've got to do it now," he said.

In his book *Map of the Soul—7,* Murray Stein predicted this turning

point in the band's journey. He wrote that the titular album was an indication that "BTS is finished with something. They are finished with a hugely creative phase," and that "BTS is... foreseeing a transformation and rebirth process." When I ask him about the band's announcement of the break, he says, "When RM said they had lost their way, I understood this to indicate the typical individuation crisis when an old identity is outgrown and a new one has not yet formed. I call this in-between phase 'liminality.' It's a period of transition, and often it is characterized as a period of drifting, experimenting, and searching for a way ahead. The BTS members are going through this phase now."

Since announcing their break, BTS have transitioned gracefully into their tenth year in 2023 with a reflective celebration of their journey as a group, closing this first chapter with their anthology album, *Proof*—a three-disk project released in June 2022 comprising lead singles, favorite tracks chosen by BTS members, and various demos and previously unreleased tracks—and beginning the next with opportunities for individual expression. Members have released solo singles and albums, each revealing different (and sometimes surprising) sides to themselves, including Jin's shimmering, upbeat single "The Astronaut"; RM's reflective and sonically diverse *Indigo* (the album opens with the lines "Fuck the trendsetter / I'ma turn back the time / back the time, far to when I was nine"); j-hope's restless, searching *Jack in the Box* ("Where's my safe zone?"); Jimin's *Face* (a portrait of his pandemic experiences, ranging from stripped-down folk to heartbreak-on-the-dance-floor synth pop); Jung Kook's garage-inspired single "Seven"; V's melancholic R&B-, soul-, and jazz-inspired *Layover* album; and SUGA's *D-Day*, the third release in his Agust D solo trilogy, whose title track, "AMYG-DALA," sees him confronting past traumas with astonishing, powerful intimacy. He also embarked on a solo world tour, and I was fortunate to attend one of the Oakland Arena concerts in May 2023, a stunning storytelling experience that felt more like an immersive black box theater piece or performance art than a conventional concert. If SUGA's solo track "Interlude: Shadow" from *Map of the Soul: 7* was a potent illustration of the concept of shadow, his concert felt like a captivating and uncompromising exploration of the psyche. The stage design was dark and stripped-down, punctuated by visual flourishes from pyrotechnics and strobe lights whose vertical beams resembled a cage (this and other moments implicated the audience in unsettling ways). Over the course of the evening, as SUGA journeyed through an extensive solo discography characterized by meditations on trauma, love, mental illness, fame, and societal ills, pieces of the stage broke off and floated to the ceiling; by the end of the night, the stage had been fully, starkly deconstructed, leaving cables and equipment exposed (in a way that briefly reminded me of Boltanski's earlier installations). SUGA, cutting a solitary figure on the arena floor, sang his final number, "The Last." In her review of the concert for *The Atlantic*, Lenika Cruz, to my mind the best journalist writing about BTS today, wrote of the ending:

> Then the spell was over. The moment the song ended, the house lights went up so that we could see him walking in silence offstage. No goodbye, no drawn-out thank yous and waves to the cheering audience. Not even a glance backward… people exchanged confused looks, shocked by his sudden exit. You could perhaps see this whole finale as a quiet confrontation with an audience, a grand assertion of the self by a beloved artist. But if it was a confrontation, it was one rooted in trust rather than condescension. Trust that the audience can sit with discomfort, that they're self-aware enough not to be offended or horrified by what he's showing them.

Over twenty-seven performances, ten cities, and two continents, SUGA ended the concert this way. But for the final encore performance in Seoul, on August 6, 2023, SUGA concluded the night by walking toward a white door spotlit on the stage. After opening it, he paused on its threshold and turned toward the audience with a smile and wave before passing through and closing it behind him. Fans realized that all this time, the concert stage had been meant to echo the set in the "AMYGDALA" music video, which sees SUGA desperately trapped in a spare, dark void of a room with a locked white door while tormented by flashes of past traumas. That he chose to end his tour with this final, liberatory statement of healing, and the symbolic closing of a life chapter, not only offers emotional narrative satisfaction but is also a testament to the patience he brings to his storytelling, which wouldn't be possible without the mutual trust he has with his fans.

At the time of writing, SUGA is preparing to begin his mandatory South Korean military service. Several members (Jin and j-hope) have already begun theirs, and others are soon to follow. The timeline is unclear, though BTS have spoken of a hoped-for reunion in 2025.

I never could have predicted becoming a BTS fan. Or that becoming a fan would reconnect me with an early artistic influence in Boltanski; with a guide to knowing myself and others better in Jung; with previous versions of myself (not just twenty-year-old art student me but also, yes, inner-child me) with whom I can resume a gentle, curious dialogue; and with a sense of connection with a vast, diverse, and deeply engaged community. Jung would call all this "synchronicity"—a meaningful coincidence of events, one inner and psychic, the other outer and physical. ARMYs would call it "BTS finding you when you need them the most." I'll let Boltanski have a word in, too: he once said of his work, "I accept all interpretations." Mostly, as all of this converges with this new, uncertain chapter, it feels like a chance to live an even deeper, bigger life than I'd previously thought possible.

Meanwhile, through their solo endeavors, and their time away from the spotlight, each member of BTS— RM (Kim Namjoon), Jin (Kim Seokjin), SUGA (Min Yoongi), j-hope (Jung Hoseok), Jimin (Park Jimin), V (Kim Taehyung), and Jung Kook (Jeon Jung Kook)—is exploring different ways to continue their path of individuation, to understand and express themselves more meaningfully, more fully, as human beings and as artists. I'll be cheering them on—and myself, and all of us out here striving for wholeness. ✱

JEREMY GAUDET

— IN CONVERSATION WITH —

RYAN H. WALSH

[MUSICIANS]

Movies and actors trapped inside Kiwi Jr. songs:
Julie Andrews
Tomb Raider
Amy Adams
The Ghost Writer

Since 2019, the Toronto band Kiwi Jr.—guitarist-vocalist Jeremy Gaudet, drummer Brohan Moore, bassist Mike Walker, and guitarist Brian Murphy, who all hail from Prince Edward Island, Canada—have crafted three albums full of punchy pop hooks and real rock riffs. As a lyricist, Gaudet kicks around familiar turns of phrase until they take on unexpected meanings: "We can forgive but we can't forget. / No, not when no one shuts up about it," he sings on "Salary Man." Their debut, Football Money *(Mint Records), was described by* The Big Takeover *as "precisely the type of record that materializes when a band actually prioritizes songwriting," and their last two albums,* Cooler Returns *and* Chopper, *released by Sub Pop, have won even greater acclaim. They scratch a particular indie-rock itch—the funny-but-rocking kind—perfected by mid-'90s titans like Guided By Voices (GBV) and Pavement, both of whom Kiwi Jr. opened for this past year.*

I spoke to Gaudet in summer 2023, between tours to promote Chopper. *A few months later, I saw Kiwi Jr. open for GBV in Dayton, Ohio, where the band managed*

Illustrations by Kristian Hammerstad

to capture attention, applause, and new fans, even as Robert Pollard's devotees waited for their hero to take the stage.
—*Ryan H. Walsh*

I. SWEATING OUT MEDIA

RYAN H. WALSH: You're in Toronto?

JEREMY GAUDET: That's right, yeah.

RHW: Where are you right now in the writing, touring, recording cycle of it all?

JG: Where we are, where I am, and where I'm supposed to be are three different things. We're still kind of touring the last album, *Chopper*, just because the way we work is we tour on weekends. Most bands might play sixty shows to promote a record. We're just stretching that out over multiple seasons.

RHW: How does songwriting work, band-wise? Are you bringing in a skeleton of a song—chords, a melody, lyrics—and then it expands from there? Or is another band member handing you some chords?

JG: It's so different for every record. For the last album I just made ten demos myself with fully fleshed-out keyboard parts and all the lyrics already done and the chords and stuff. And then I brought it to the band and we took things apart and put them back together and things changed to an extent, but that record was largely constructed in the demo phase.

RHW: Do you have notebooks full of potential lyrics and titles that you use as raw material?

JG: More or less. In college, a long time ago, I would use a notebook, thinking it was very authorly of me, as if I was tapping into some kind of creative archetype. Now I just use my phone, and people are a lot less weirded out.

RHW: There's that funny moment where you're like, Would my writing be better if I bought this thirty-dollar Moleskine or typed it all out on an old typewriter? I think everyone has to confront that moment of pretentiousness and fight it. I have a never-ending Notes app with, like, a lyrics database, and I'll pop in there and see if anything screams at me on a particular day. And you're not weird doing that, like you said; you're just like everybody else. You can be a stranger on a train who's working on lyrics but it looks like you're texting friends.

JG: I was once scolded at a party. Somebody said something I thought was just really funny and I was like, Oh, I've got to remember this dialogue I'm hearing, and I ran over to my schoolbag to get a notebook. Somebody followed me and was like, "Put it back in the bag. Don't do it."

RHW: Seems harsh. Let someone write something down! Who cares! You're a great songwriter, but you also seem interested in all kinds of writing. It pops up again and again in your lyrics: novels, screenplays. The concept of a nearly drowned person, still soaking wet, asking someone to read their screenplay [in the song "The Sound of Music"] is super funny to me.

JG: I don't know that I'm aware of that, really. I took creative writing at university and stuff and, well, I'm a librarian now.

RHW: Oh, well, that's a great answer: "librarian." You breathe it. You're literally surrounded.

JG: Somebody was asking me once about all the movie references on the new album, and in my mind, I knew there were a few, but then somebody laid out a list of all these moments. They confronted me with it and I was unaware of it. When you see it all laid out in front of you—and it's like, *Explain this*—it's hard. [*Both laugh.*] The only thing I could think of was that, during two years in lockdown in Canada, I consumed a lot of media, and it just started to sweat out of me.

RHW: You could say that these years we didn't really live a full life, but we lived the movies and TV shows we watched. Not to get all—

JG: I have a theory that when you run into people over a certain age, you end up talking about the weather, obviously, but if you run into people your own age or younger, you end up talking about TV shows within the first few lines back and forth.

RHW: *Yeah, it was kind of sunny today. Have you seen...* On that topic, in your opinion, has a movie or TV show ever done a good job at showing the process of writing? They love to make the main character a writer, but when it comes down to showing the process of writing, they have to avoid it, or often it's super boring. Has it been done well? That's my question.

JG: Do you know a movie I like… What the fuck is that guy's name? Pierce Brosnan is in it. Oh yeah, *The Ghost Writer*. Did you see that? He plays the prime minister. And Ewan McGregor is hired to ghostwrite his memoir, and he slowly starts to realize that the *previous* ghostwriter was murdered for uncovering something. It's a pretty good movie.

RHW: By the way, I wanted to go back to a previous point. I like when someone notices a grand theme or repetition in something I made that I didn't notice. Did you enjoy that moment when your movie references were compiled, or did you find it kind of like *Oh no, I've been caught here!*

JG: I like it. If anything, just because people are paying enough attention.

RHW: Totally. A lot of your lyrics are very funny and I really love those laugh lines. But the thing is, they're not funny *songs*. You wouldn't play your songs on *Dr. Demento* or whatever. Do you know what *Dr. Demento* is?

JG: No, I just like the way it sounds.

RHW: It was this unhinged radio show where this old kook in a top hat would play novelty songs. Anyway, you do this really delicate tightrope walk, where there are funny lines but the songs still always have emotional weight. Do you strive to make sure both those things are in balance?

JG: I'm pretty deliberate with that stuff. I spend way more time on the lyrics than we as a band do, practicing the songs and getting them ready. I guess it's just a way of me being kind of selfish and just putting things I would like to hear or see into songs.

RHW: Yes! If you're not making stuff that you wish existed, then what are you even doing? Have you ever revised a song and thought, Whoops, this reads like a joke book.

JG: I would say the opposite is more often true, where I have a fear that something's coming across far more sincere than I would like it to, or just kind of not in keeping with the spirit of who we are as a band. Do you remember when Blink-182 was dominating the world in 2002, or whenever that was?

RHW: What a special time.

JG: They put out "Adam's Song," this super slow song about suicide, and it was the follow-up to, I don't know, when they were running around naked in their videos and stuff. I don't know why I'm talking about Blink-182, but I just mean the equivalent of that. I'm cautious about that.

RHW: But it's funny you say "more sincere," because I find in all your songs, even if they're funny, you're not just rolling your eyes and sneering. They're getting to a point of view that seems unique and legitimate to me.

JG: Yeah, that's something I'm aware of too. We get channeled with these—I don't want to say any names—but there's some slacker rock bands that I really have nothing in common with. When I think of my songs and other groups' songs, just from what we set out to do as a band, the way we want to sound, some of the comparison stuff is so artificial.

RHW: One of the first things I learned, growing up in the '90s and then starting a band in the early '00s, was that you can't run a band if you're a mess. The slacker thing was a total myth because either they're working super hard behind the scenes or someone else around them has to do all the hard work. *Someone* is working their ass off. So it just immediately

Janis Joplin

rang so phony to me that that was a viable form of a successful creative person, the slacker.

JG: I once read an interview with someone from Interpol. The interviewer was roasting the band for wearing coordinated suits or whatever they did on *Letterman*, and that Interpol guy asked the interviewer something like *Do you think that more work went into us all buying the same suit, or a band like Pavement making sure nobody's wearing the same shorts?* Something like that. And I think it's pretty true. Everything's calculated to an extent.

II. "A SHORT, PLEASANT BRAIN VIRUS"

RHW: When you got that out-of-the-blue email from Sub Pop with interest in your band, was there a second when you thought it was a prank?

JG: No, because it was just a nice personal email. There was no contract or anything.

RHW: *I'm flying the contract to you right now! You have thirty minutes to sign!*

JG: *There's a limo outside—I'll explain everything!*

RHW: We've gone over TV and movies. Do you like poetry? Do you read it? Do you have any poets you like?

JG: Yeah, for sure. I don't read anything anymore, because I'm a total lazy, terrible person, but when I do, I'll usually just pick up a book and read a couple of poems. I like Mark Leidner, Rachel B. Glaser, Natalie Shapero. I have old guys that everybody likes: James Tate, Jack Gilbert. You?

RHW: David Berman led me to John Ashbery, and I went through everything he published. It's the closest I've ever come to gold panning. It's like he starts every poem literally not knowing if it's going anywhere special, and when it does, the surprise and wonder become like an electric presence in the room. I think it genuinely surprised him, too, when it happened. I always picture him casually hobbling away from his typewriter, going, *Oh wow, that turned out pretty neat.*

I always know it's great poetry if I walk away from it and start thinking about the world around me with the same logic found in the poem. Like a short, pleasant brain virus. Some poems instantly lead me to more interesting thought patterns. That's a pretty astounding result for a medium that is essentially considered useless by the majority of the population.

How about the age-old question: Do you care if your lyrics stand up on the page without music?

JG: I once saw GZA give a talk at my university [McGill in Montreal], and I wanted to ask him that, because he's a super cerebral dude and a great writer. But I waited too long to get the courage to go up to the mic [during the Q&A], and within forty-five seconds, 150 white dudes got in line. *Yeah, man, just want to know if you have any advice for young rappers trying to get started.* So I wanted to ask GZA that, and I never did.

As for me, I don't know. Obviously, I write my lyrics down, and go over them to make sure they can stand up on their own on the page. A lot of songwriters collect their lyrics and put them out. Jarvis Cocker did a book; I think Billy Corgan did too. We did that with our record *Cooler Returns*. We made a comic book. Just all the lyrics. And we got illustrators to do these great drawings for each song, but that was just, like, a pandemic project, when we couldn't play and we had time and wanted to have something to put out.

RHW: I have a few of those collected lyrics books, but often I'll go to them only because I'm listening to the song. I feel like it's a bit of a myth that people are just sitting down completely divorced from the music that the lyrics came from and reading it like it's a novel.

JG: No, I'm trying to imagine if I could ever read lyrics and just not hear that person's voice singing them.

RHW: You said this in an interview about the cover art for *Chopper*, the latest album: "I wrote this big essay about it to convince the other guys in the band about it. Without getting too into it, it just sort of fit." I really relate hard to that as a person who's written essay-type things to convince his band to do something. [*Laughs*]

JG: I don't know if you saw the press release or whatever for *Chopper*? It's on our website. It's a heavily edited version of the giant email I sent to convince everyone.

RHW: I read that and thought, Wait a second. This is the press release, but it's strange and compelling. Who wrote this and what's the purpose? I wondered if the press got mad that there was no useful factual information in there. Did you get any feedback?

JG: So we did one for each of our previous records, and they're inspired by—you know how Bob Dylan had crazy stuff on the back of his LPs? Sort of in that vein. I collaborate with a friend of mine from grad school named Mark. He contributes a lot to those. We did three of those big weird press release things, and I don't know if anyone read them.

RHW: I did.

JG: We usually send those out when we announce the album, and then the label also has their own more standard press release that just gets to the facts that most people want to see.

RHW: We all know how boring the "Who are your influences?" question is, but can you name a band or an artist that is super removed from what you do, or from the sound you have, from whom you learned something vital?

JG: I'm not sure this is that far removed from the suspected influences of a Canadian songwriter, but maybe in the indie-rock sphere it is: Gordon Lightfoot. I heard his music a lot growing up—my dad's a huge fan and had all the records—but I didn't connect with his music until a few years ago, around the time Kiwi Jr. was writing or preparing to write our second album, *Cooler Returns*. There's such craftsmanship to how he wrote songs. He would handwrite the full notation, even the vocal melodies, so the song is down on paper for the official record. Serious songwriter stuff. You get the impression that one word or one note sung differently would ruin it for him.

I've tried to take the approach of making every word matter. Even if, sometimes, it would feel so good to start a bunch of lines in a verse with "And so—" Lightfoot was that kind of writer where there's no wasted words. I will still mess around while performing songs live and change certain lines on a whim, but I'm quite certain it's not a great idea, and I don't think anybody likes it when you do that, unless you're Dylan.

RHW: And were there unlikely influences that led specifically to the sound of *Chopper*?

JG: Because our goal was to make a "nighttime"-sounding album, we made a playlist of all the songs we thought captured the vibe we were going for. Songs that hit 100 percent only when they're played late at night and bring a certain vibe that's mysterious, romantic, and sort of cinematic. The playlist was called "Michael Mann presents Kiwi Jr.," and we had some things in our wheelhouse like *This Night*–era Destroyer, the Clientele, Richard Hawley, but it also had a lot of songs by the Weeknd. He's from Toronto, and you can't walk into a drugstore without hearing a Weeknd song. It's either him or Drake. But I quite like the Weeknd, and a lot of the sounds we were going for on *Chopper*, while it was never said out loud, could be traced back to the new wave and '80s synth. There's an overlap between the Weeknd and '80s Rod Stewart—a sweet spot I was trying to get to.

RHW: I wish I liked the Weeknd, because he is everywhere. He's the first artist in history where both grocery stores and strip clubs agree: *This music is 100 percent for us*. Do you have any artists or genres you *wish* you liked, but that you can't seem to connect with?

JG: I like some pop music but I wish I liked everything that's popular, and could congratulate coworkers for scoring Taylor Swift tickets or whatever it is that everyone is talking about that week. Seems like fun to be a pop fan. I also see Grateful Dead fans having a lot of fun in the last, like, ten years. That band seems to still be spreading around and getting bigger. I like some of it, but I'm not able to make small talk about it with a fan.

III. "CAPITAL-D DRAMA"

RHW: Let's take the song "The Sound of Music," from your latest album. On the surface level, it has a string of references and non sequiturs, but I come away from that song feeling like I just spent time in a specific story, or with a certain group of people. Do you have that feeling? What kind of feeling or mental image does that song give you?

JG: That song, to me, is as close to a narrative song as I'd write. That song is tied up in, for lack of a better word, capital-*D*

Drama. There's a lot of calling people out for performances or calling out a specific person in the song for being overly performative.

RHW: How do Julie Andrews and the film *The Sound of Music* fit into that?

JG: It's like fan fiction. She and her husband were divorced within two years of *The Sound of Music* coming out, after being together since they were kids. I was writing a sort of narrative song about a breakup, and at some point, something clicked, and I realized it would be a lot juicier if I set the song in a world of actors—everybody being overdramatic. I think I had just read an article about Julie Andrews and Tony Walton and thought it would work to bring them into the song. You can cast whoever you want in a song. You don't need permission. There's the song "Highlights of 100" on *Cooler Returns*, with the line "Bells ring out the pouring rain / and Amy Adams rides the train," and it's the same sort of thing where I reasoned it was both more evocative and more effective to plop somebody into the song rather than try and create some character in the half a second I'm giving myself in the verse to talk about it. I'm just saying, *OK, picture Amy Adams on a train while it's raining and church bells are going off*, and that's the taking-off point.

IV. "HEY, I SAID THAT!"

RHW: I really loved hearing that you and other band members are perfectly fine communicating that you all have day jobs and need to do the majority of your touring on weekends and on vacation time. It seems to me that for many years, there was great shame in artists admitting this kind of thing, which I believe had terrible effects. Does it ever surprise your fans to learn this? Do you find any advantages to being a successful band whose members also all have other work and jobs?

JG: In regards to working day jobs and telling fans that you know a lot about Microsoft Excel, I'm not sure if fans are ever weird about it, but other bands and some industry people can be. And telling your coworkers you need to take a week off because you're going to New York City to sing in front of people is weird. I've walked a tightrope for years, hoping people don't Google Image–search my name and see me

with a guitar and wearing a type of shirt they haven't seen me wear before. I think at this point everyone knows I play music and they just agree to not bring it up to me, because I've been so weird about it.

It's like I'm a cheating husband. I have excuses about going to Philadelphia to "visit cousins" or taking a trip to Boston with "the guys." I had a job at a law firm years ago and someone found out I played in a band. They sent out an email to all the employees about a gig we were playing and made it a company outing. Playing to twenty of your coworkers in the front row is why I never tell anyone anything anymore.

RHW: Nightmare. Earlier we talked about the Notes app on your smartphone facilitating an invisible, unpretentious way of working on lyrics in public. Have you ever included something a friend said in a song that they later identified? Like, *Hey, I said that!*

JG: I have whole songs based on anecdotes people have told me. The line in "Parasite II" about being in denial about gaining weight, and claiming somebody was shrinking all your shirts in the laundry—my friend Christian said that in a serious tone one night. I'm not sure I ever told him that it made it into a song. The second verse of "The Extra Sees the Film" is a friend's story of coming across a car wreck in a snowstorm while on the way to playing a gig in a country band. They were looking for bodies in the snow but had to leave to make their set. He's probably heard the song, but he hasn't said anything yet.

RHW: Reminds me of my favorite line from Bowie's "Five Years": "Don't think you knew you were in the song." Haunting. Any others?

JG: From "Cooler Returns," there's the line "I don't want to task you out, but can you break this five for the jukebox, Jodi?" Mike [the bassist] said this to Jodi [a bartender] at a pub in our neighborhood, and we all laughed at the ridiculous turn of phrase and knew it was gonna be in a song. I have never heard somebody say, "I don't want to task you out, but..." before or since.

The song "Only Here for a Haircut" is a true story. My friend's girlfriend would give me haircuts every once in a while, and one day I went over and asked her for a haircut and my friend wasn't there and she was being kinda weird. *Tomb Raider* was on the TV, and I pieced together during the haircut that they had just broken up that morning, so she was just cutting her ex-boyfriend's friend's hair for some reason. They recognized the song immediately when they heard it.

V. BOSTON LOVE

RHW: Kiwi Jr. played Boston in February of 2023, which was the first time I saw the band live. Near the end, you remarked on how weird the audience was, and that you all needed to get out of there as soon as possible. I could tell you were joking, but there was something sincere about it as well. As a native Bostonian, I'd love to go over the details there.

JG: We got to the area with a few hours to kill before the venue opened, so we went to a sports bar and got wings and beer. They had televisions above the urinals and a big old-style boxing bell they'd ring every once in a while. After a couple of hours, the Bruins game had ended and we needed to leave. We split up and wandered around, bumping into each other every two minutes.

RHW: Like a Three Stooges bit.

JG: I didn't know if we had any fans in Boston. They knew our music, but it seemed like they didn't want us to know they were fans. They'd go from singing along to heckling to trying to bring us drinks to trying to grab the mic from me. It was like playing to a crowd of in-character extras from *Pirates of the Caribbean*. We're very familiar with an Irish/Scottish beer-drunk crowd, but this show had a different weirdness to it. Somebody brought their own tambourine to play. Another guy kept trying to tell me jokes in between songs. It was also all men, and I think most of them felt like they were waiting to be discovered.

RHW: OK, I can clear some of this up. Singing along *and* also heckling means we loved it but were afraid that if we showed you too much appreciation you'd never come back. You got Boston-loved. This all sounds fairly normal to me. But you're also interviewing a fish about water here. One of my very first times onstage at a bar with a band, we were ceaselessly heckled the entire set by a one-armed-man.

Regarding the tambourine man, I was near that guy in the audience. He was hammered and picked up the opening band's tambourine. Valid complaint. He also kept yelling "Start Choppin'" at you between songs, which I just now realized he did because the guitarist in the opening band was wearing a Dinosaur Jr. shirt and he thought requesting a Dino Jr. song from another "Jr." band was funny. It was eventually funny to me in the sense of how dumbly dedicated to that bit he was all night. It started before you plugged in and went till the end. But that crowd loved the show. You were great. It could have been worse, right?

JG: We just got back from a European tour. During sound check in Amsterdam, my amp was making a strange noise, like a big electrical crackle. We spent a long time trying out various cables and testing pedals. Eventually, we thought it might be my shoes? When I played in sock feet it was fine, but when I put my sneakers on, the big crackle came back instantly. It had something to do with the rubber on the bottoms maybe shielding some type of static. Also playing North American gear through EU power is always freaky. So we finally figure this out, but I need to wear something on my feet because I have some guitar pedals with buttons on them that you can't really click with a bare foot. We go on in twenty minutes, so I'm running around Amsterdam going into sneaker stores, but everything is like four hundred euros. We were in the Sneaker District. It was all designer shit. I'm going in and out of stores, asking for their cheapest pair, but I can't find anything under a hundred and fifty euros. With five minutes to go, I grab a pair of slides at a drugstore. But I get the wrong size and they won't stay on my feet. So I wrap them in tape just in time to make our stage call. I go on and pick up my guitar and the amp instantly crackles, like the shoes made no difference at all. After the show I can't get the tape off. I'm trying to cut it off with my keys. The band Protomartyr walked by our dressing room laughing at me, like, *What the hell are you doing?* I bought some nice sneakers a day later in Utrecht and they also made the noise. So it's not the sneakers; it's me. ★

106

GENTLE CONFRONTATION

BY LORAINE JAMES

When people began to associate dance music with social lowliness in the early '90s, London clubs moved away from a night of dancing as their primary selling point, and instead touted a more atmospheric kind of electronic music that came to be known as intelligent dance music (IDM). One of the most prominent criticisms waged against the genre since then highlights the whiteness of its early creators. Thirty years in, Loraine James has become an unlikely champion of IDM—even though, as she notes, her music isn't often categorized as such, because she's a Black woman.

James's discography at different times seems to speak to the various phases of IDM's history, each of which moved the genre closer to the brash, danceable music it first reacted to, with the latest phase marking what music writer Simon Reynolds calls the assimilation of "the rudeboy spirit of rave itself." On *Building Something Beautiful for Me* (2022), an album celebrating Black composer Julius Eastman, James seems to pay tribute to IDM's ambient beginnings, whereas her 2019 album, *For You and I*, is in that quintessential hard-to-dance-to-but-still-quite-danceable IDM territory I associate most with second-wave IDM.

On *Gentle Confrontation*, released in September 2023, James edges her way toward the world of pop and other mainstream music like rap and R&B. Don't get me wrong: if we're in R&B territory, we're in deconstructed R&B territory—you might hear the likes of Mhysa or Actress here too. This isn't a vibrant hyperpop moment, not a total mirror of IDM's recent reverse acceleration back into the spirit of the nightclub, but it does mark a version of James that seems both more playful and more adult at the same time.

The more-adult James we get on *Gentle Confrontation* is actually a tribute to her teenage self. As on *For You and I*, we return to her childhood home, the Alma Estate, to ruminate once again on James's coming-of-age. This is the backdrop for the musician's continued exploration of her queer sexuality, the death of her father at age seven, and her genesis as a musician. *Gentle Confrontation* also takes up the rhythmic inclinations of *For You and I*, and to great effect, but the overall sound is further developed in this later album because of the way it more deeply incorporates teenage Loraine's influences—math rock and emo.

Some critics, like Tope Olufemi, recognize the "wonky time signatures and complex melodies" of math rock in James's earlier work. But others struggle to hear any similarity to the emo bands she has always loved, such as American Football. It's as if the eighth track on *Gentle Confrontation*, "One Way Ticket to the Midwest (Emo)," were a direct response to this. In an interview about a 2022 release under James's other moniker, Under the Weather, music journalist Philip Sherburne said, "I have to admit that I don't really hear any emo influence in the record!" "Yeah, I guess you wouldn't," responded James (in my mind, I can hear her sigh dejectedly). "But I've always been inspired by emo."

Gentle Confrontation is James's best album, too, because we see James make better use of her vocalists. While listening to "Déjà Vu," I find myself thinking about what a great instrumentalist James is, even as featured vocalist RiTchie produces a sexy, low, and rumbling performance. James shows off how well she can complement a singer's voice without overwhelming it. Throughout the album, James and her vocalists are in dynamic alignment. It's *Gentle Confrontation*'s strength as a vocally oriented album that, in addition to making a contribution to the field of deconstructed R&B, should be read as a blueprint for IDMers who have a vested interest in stretching what "intelligent" sounds like.

All in all, fans of James will be delighted by *Gentle Confrontation*. Just make sure you have good equipment on hand for listening. James is working the middle and low frequencies in deliciously complex ways that you'll miss out on without a proper set of speakers. —*Anaïs Duplan*

> Record label: *Hyperdub* Similar artists: *Tirzah, Squarepusher, Oli XL* Representative lyric: *"I want the ride, I don't want to arrive."* Best track: *"I DM U"* Ideal listening conditions: *Nighttime walk under baseball field lights*

Illustration by Pete Gamlen

A TIME TO LOVE, A TIME TO DIE

BY AMOR MUERE

Someone asked me once, in a tone of complete ordinariness, what the difference is between noise and sound. We were in the Museo Soumaya, in Mexico City, on that top floor cluttered with Rodin sculptures (purchased and hauled there by the Mexican billionaire Carlos Slim). The question incited a muteness in me, one that suited the room full of motionless figures and their bronze, certain light. I was beginning to love her, the asker of this futile question. I told her I didn't know, but I'd go searching for a worthwhile response. But of course this never came to pass. Of course, by the time I'd finally discovered the words to bring to her, she was gone.

If there is a border between noise and sound, it is crossed over many times by the Mexico City–based experimental collective Amor Muere. The group is made of four musicians: Camille Mandoki, Concepción Huerta, Gibrana Cervantes, and Mabe Fratti—two classically trained instrumentalists and two electronic-music artists. Their songs are the composite of many tones: violin and cello, vocals, synthesizers, tape manipulation, and other sonic fabrications, all housed within a single soundscape. Times collide—the classic and the contemporary—producing a momentary glimpse of music's tall history. We are met, as listeners, with a stockpiling of sound: utterly beautiful, love-ridden, unafraid to trespass into discordance.

Amor Muere's first album, *A Time to Love, a Time to Die*, is composed of just five songs, which feel almost like five movements of a single piece. Each track, like the movements of a requiem, repeats one or more melodic motifs. But this album is not a requiem, though it has death in its title, and though I imagined calling it a requiem before I heard it. It is too precarious, too wandering—it is too restless to be a song for granting rest. These are love songs and grief songs; songs that travel from the chaos of noise to the solidity of sound, but songs that never

Record label: *Scrawl* **Similar artists:** *Organ Tapes, Eartheater, Elysia Crampton* **Representative lyric:** *"I went out and bought some air."* **Best track:** *"Can we provoke reciprocal reaction"* **Ideal listening conditions:** *Cooking on low heat*

abandon the meaningless passion and delirium of noise.

Amor Muere made the majority of their album while gathered at one member's home in Zoncuantla, Veracruz. Often their songs began in improvisational sessions, and a good portion of the project was recorded live. As a consequence, one experiences them being made as you listen to them. *A Time to Love, a Time to Die* presents music in flux, music in desperate search of its own shape.

There is technical expertise on great display in this project. The string playing, in particular, is magnificent. The production is clear as daylight, of the highest order. But technique alone will never make a love song, let alone a grief song. I feel, in a distinct way, that real love and heartbreak were placed into the machine of these five eerie and nomadic songs. Paul Robeson once said, "A singer must also be an expert at living." Things were lived for this music to be born; lovers standing in silence, questions and answers never meeting.

I wrote to the members of Amor Muere and asked them the question I was asked years ago near the statues: What is the difference between noise and sound? "We think noise is a type of sound," they replied, "[but] it's hard to talk about the difference. Could you rephrase the question?"

Of course, I couldn't.

"Music started out from noise. After a long journey, it's going back home," wrote Hernan Diaz at the end of his most recent novel, *Trust*. Maybe it is through listening to this album that I finally understand his line, though I've loved it—without understanding it at all—for many months now. Noise is a type of sound, and formlessness a kind of form. I love the amorous, ethereal songs Amor Muere has made for us. They are documents of music losing and finding its figure. They are records of music going back home.

—Ricardo Frasso Jaramillo

Illustration by Pete Gamlen

MEAT JOY

BY MEAT JOY

It was Austin, Texas, in the middle of the Reagan era. There were Klan marches (and far larger counterprotests) on the Capitol, and the Republican National Convention set up shop a few hours away in Dallas. It was three years before the inaugural SXSW festival, which would eventually cement the city's reputation as an industry-friendly international music destination. Meat Joy released their only full-length album, a joyful and defiant and uniquely Texan self-titled LP, in 1984.

Austin in 1984 might have been contradictory, but it was also affordable and exploding with eccentric creativity. Daniel Johnston was in the midst of a magical run of home-recorded cassettes, and the avant-garde rockers the Butthole Surfers were practicing what their drummer dubbed "Texas drag" (adopting stereotypical Texas drawls and clothing in service of subversion). Meat Joy's Jamie Spidle remembers this Austin fondly: show flyers for imaginary bands littered the UT campus, and teenagers with boom boxes breakdanced on cardboard outside his band's two-hundred-dollar-a-month warehouse rehearsal space.

All this chaos and activism and messy DIY spirit made its way onto *Meat Joy*. The band members, largely queer art and theater kids who operated as a leaderless collective, were intent on destroying the fourth wall at their shows. They passed instruments out into the crowd and held after-show art parties where friends and fans helped make their next batch of custom album covers. When it came to recording, that all-in spirit persisted: each member of Meat Joy served as "captain" of a handful of songs on the album, directing the arrangements and guiding their own sound. "We liked each other as friends and people so much that we were open to embracing whatever each of us brought to the band," Mellissa DeMille recalled. "The friendship provided the freedom."

The resulting record is a sonic documentary that captures Meat Joy and the kinetic Austin underground in equal measure. It opens with a moody lo-fi instrumental chamber piece, improvised on cello, recorder, and violin—an instrument that Spidle had never picked up before recording the track. "Prelude in Cb" has the qualities of both a regal orchestra tune-up and a pair of seagulls fighting over an abandoned ham sandwich. The angular studio-recorded punk sing-along "Another Pair" rails against the objectification of women. If those opening songs seem to exist in entirely different aural universes, there are more to come: Gretchen Phillips's kid brother hollering over a discordant children's glockenspiel; a twenty-three-second excerpt of Tim Mateer's earnest strumming and singing on "Questions"; shards of sampled TV ads; a very Texan honky-tonk campfire instrumental called "Last Round Up."

None of which is to say that Meat Joy lacked thematic coherence. The band, named after a performance art piece by experimental artist Carolee Schneemann, had a shared interest in fighting sexism, violence, and homophobia. "For When Love Is Irrelevance" is a propulsive and pissed-off piece about normalized forms of sexual abuse; the dark and distorted "Proud to Be Stupid" lampoons the violent jocks at the fringe of the punk scene; the anxious "Pleasure Time" eulogizes that "it's not safe on the dance floor anymore." The twangy punk anthem "Slenderella" approaches anorexia in full Texas drag, despite the band's barely concealed rage at conditions that make eating disorders commonplace.

These are songs of resistance and community that belong to a very specific time and place, but all the band's youthful anger feels eerily familiar in the post-Roe America of book bans and anti-trans laws. In celebration of the album's fortieth anniversary and reissue, Meat Joy's members have been prepping for a pair of reunion shows. It's a joyful process with a hint of melancholy. "I'm very proud of our work," DeMille said. "And sad that we still fight the war on sexism, racism, homophobia, and transphobia... We must keep reweaving the tapestry of our society to ensure that all of us are woven in and that there are no *others*."

—*Casey Jarman*

> **Record label:** *Flesh & Blood Music* **Similar artists:** *the Slits, the Au Pairs, Bratmobile, Bongwater* **Representative lyric:** *"Every man is born with a weapon. / Every man has his tool."* **Best track:** *"Final Curtain"* **Ideal listening conditions:** *With friends, at a large kitchen table, making collaborative art*

Illustration by Pete Gamlen

ROCKSTAR

BY DOLLY PARTON

In 1977, a flurry of publicity brought the news that country superstar Dolly Parton—already famous for her songs "Jolene" and "I Will Always Love You"—was crossing over to the mainstream. Alanna Nash's intensively reported book *Dolly* documents this moment as a rancorous one, reminiscent of Dylan going electric. Repeatedly, Parton is prompted to align herself with a genre. "I really prefer to call it Dolly Parton's music," she says to Nash. "Why should it have a label?" Rock, she tells another interviewer, "was something I'd wanted to do for years, but I wasn't in a position to.... I don't necessarily want to be a rock and roll star, but I want to be able to go into any market, to express myself totally."

By then, the popularity of Parton's songs with bona fide female rock stars like Patti Smith and Tina Turner had finally put her in such a position. Yet Parton's crossover attempt ultimately failed to find advocacy from rock critics. *The Village Voice*'s Robert Christgau quipped, "The problem with Dolly's crossover is her rich but rather tiny voice, a singular country treble that's unsuited to rock, where little-girlishness works only as an occasional novelty." *Rolling Stone*'s Tom Carson was more brutal: "Outside the stylized [country and western] framework, her voice and stance seem ludicrous." Subpar material (1978's disco-tinged *Heartbreaker*) was their primary complaint, but judgment was also cast on Parton herself: her musical talents had their charms, but they didn't quite measure up to real rock stardom.

This brazenly sexist and obliquely classist reception did not stop Parton from continuing to record rock music. Just as other artists kept embracing her songwriting, she showed discernment in choosing others' songs to interpret, with often intriguing results. In 1979, she rendered the Beatles' "Help!" as a brisk, airy ballad; 1980's concept album *9 to 5 and Odd Jobs* explores folk rock with moving versions of Woody Guthrie's "Deportee (Plane Wreck at Los Gatos)" and "The House of the Rising Sun." And especially exciting rock experiments came with 2001's *Little Sparrow*, recorded with the innovative bluegrass band Nickel Creek. Daringly tackling Collective Soul's grunge-era classic "Shine," Parton's voice is confident and clear as a crystal bell. Though she's accompanied by banjo, mandolin, and fiddle, it's pretty evident that she rocks.

So what does an artist once deemed "unsuited to rock" sing on an album called *Rockstar*, fresh from her 2022 induction into the Rock and Roll Hall of Fame and joined by everyone from Melissa Etheridge to Kid Rock? Along with a few songs of her own, the biggest hits by the most fixed bodies in the rock firmament seem a fair place to start. *Rockstar* does indeed include a bunch of classic-rock anthems by the likes of the Beatles, the Rolling Stones, Led Zeppelin, Peter Frampton, and Lynyrd Skynyrd; it also highlights a few more subversive and stylistically groundbreaking rock icons, including Prince, Stevie Nicks, Heart, and Queen.

Aside from the symbolic import of its selections, the music of *Rockstar* shows the same thoughtfulness and precision found elsewhere in Parton's work. She seeks neither to replicate nor to radically transform these songs, and instead subtly yet convincingly reimagines them.

"Let It Be" is exemplary of this method. Paul McCartney's performance of perhaps his most famous song has always been emotionally cool, suggesting a stoic detachment from its depiction of divine or dreamlike solace. As if sensing that distance, Parton's version moves in closely. With a stately pace, the reassuring sweetness of her tone, and (ace up her sleeve at least since "I Will Always Love You") a spoken-word refrain, its more vulnerable and spiritual register opens up the song.

This delicate dynamic between source material and interpretation reminds us of Parton's brilliance as a musician, still frequently misunderstood or underestimated—her vocal control, her phrasing, her sense of compositional form, and her joyful, engaged approach to collaboration. And so *Rockstar* cannily defines rock stardom not by a fixed sound or attitude, but by the idealistic, demanding terms Parton set for herself decades ago: having the freedom to express yourself, totally. —*Emma Ingrisani*

Record label: *Butterfly/Big Machine* Similar artists: *Linda Ronstadt, Emmylou Harris, Johnny Cash, Tina Turner, Nickel Creek* Representative lyric: *"Whisper words of wisdom, / let it be."* Best track: *"Let It Be"* Ideal listening conditions: *An early-morning walk on a clear day*

Illustration by Pete Gamlen

WATER MADE US

BY JAMILA WOODS

Five tracks into Jamila Woods's third studio album, *Water Made Us*, halfway through "Send a Dove," the synthetic beat fades and Woods pleads, "Don't raise your voice at me. / I'll flinch like it's a fist. / You're so quick to rage. / You know I hate to fear you."

The song reveals all Woods's talents as a singer, songwriter, and storyteller: profundity through vulnerability, spirituality, bop-ability, a swaying cadence that lifts the listener toward epiphany. There is a haunting emotional buoyancy that only the best artists can transfer to their listeners. The song contains a melding of sender and receiver, making the listener feel the fear.

Before the beat fades, the album knocks like a friend at your door asking to sit down, reflecting on a recent breakup, wondering if she's happy; wondering, as in "Bugs," "Will I ever settle down? Will I turn my life around?" Woods allows herself to succumb to initial love flutters, but in "Tiny Garden" she accepts that this relationship is not "gonna be a big production." "It's gonna be a tiny garden, but I'll feed it every day."

There are small joys on this album: the smiling sounds of fresh love and the faith that it could maybe work out. There is acceptance in "Practice"—the acknowledgment that some relationships are meant solely to prepare you, train you, and get you ready for the rest of your life.

Through the first four songs and an interlude, Woods is on our couch, telling us the story over a bottle of wine or whiskey, a joint, pausing occasionally to dance. She is prepared for the breakup. She has accepted it. She understands, in her chest and in her prayers, that this relationship isn't right. There is a break. There are tarot cards and candlelight.

Then we enter the album's beautifully and brutally complex "Send a Dove," where there is confusion, jumbled emotions, a smooth and bopping beat over sweet poetry.

Loyal fans of Woods will recognize in *Water Made Us* the

hallmarks of her maturing style. This album is covered in spirituality (the flood, the doves). The writing is superb.

The title was inspired by a Toni Morrison quote about the Mississippi River flooding.

"In fact," Ms. Morrison once said at a New York Public Library event, "it is not flooding: it is remembering." Unlike Woods's gorgeous song "Sula," released in 2020 and named after Morrison's classic novel, on *Water Made Us*, Woods is not explicitly borrowing subject matter. In this latest venture, she is pulling from her own depths, revealing herself, bare and singular. Jamila: her own inspiration.

The few guest appearances on the album are well balanced. Saba, duendita, and Peter CottonTale inject the right amount of variety while still allowing Woods to maintain a focus on herself.

The album sustains its brilliance for seventeen introspective tracks. By the middle Woods has finished her wine, whiskey, and weed, and she moves on from the initial story of a short-lived romance. She breaks out her guitar on "Wolfsheep," gives us dry, folksy, lyrical skepticism, similar to that of boygenius. She wonders, "If you shudder when they mention my name," if she "can tell between who loves and who's hunting me."

She carries her guitar into the kitchen on "Backburner," confronts her faults, tells us about "all the lovers that I got stay steaming in the pot."

At the end Woods puts down the guitar and offers us another dance break, moves around the living room as we watch from the couch, tries to pull us to our feet, keeps moving and doesn't watch the clock. "I think you really want to dance with me. / How could you really want to dance with me? / Do you really want to dance?" Yes, of course we want to dance. We want you to tell us everything.

—*Gabriel Bump*

Record label: *Jagjaguwar* **Similar artists:** *Jazmine Sullivan, boygenius, James Blake, Nai Palm, Frank Ocean, Joy Oladokun* **Representative lyric:** *"I tried to feed your hunger, until it swallowed me."* **Best track:** *"Send a Dove"* **Ideal listening conditions:** *First week of March, an unseasonably warm day, driving southbound on Lake Shore Drive*

THE PUZZLE OF INCREDIBLY WIDE AND DEEP KNOWLEDGE

IF YOU COMPLETE THIS PUZZLE, YOU ARE A GENERALIST OF BROAD SKILL AND GREAT RENOWN

by Wyna Liu; edited by Benjamin Tausig

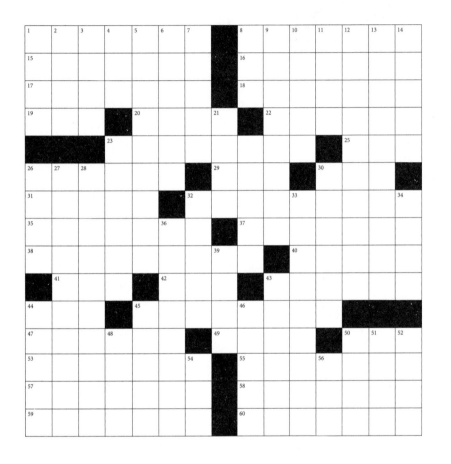

ACROSS

1. It's inserted before withdrawing
8. Wicked liquid?
15. Sport whose name derives from the Basque for "merry festival"
16. Coming
17. Mean H.S. course?
18. Hilary Hahn or Eddie Van Halen, at times
19. Quick suggestion
20. Lighter options
22. Iconic hip hop label founded in an NYU dorm room
23. Behind, but cuter
25. Peer Gynt's mother
26. Doom, for one
29. "Super Soul Musical" of 1975, with "The"
30. Actor Vigoda
31. ___ rock
32. Weave together, as contrapuntal melodies
35. Place atop
37. Proceed cautiously
38. Source of stuffiness
40. Certain Greek singer
41. One drinking to excess, archaically
42. Kurosawa film scored by Toru Takemitsu
43. Care for
44. When repeated, sound in a sci-fi fight
45. Fellini film that inspired "Mr. Tambourine Man" and "Me and Bobby McGee"
47. Hermitage
49. First Nigerian-born artist to win a Grammy (Best New Artist, 1986)
50. Goodie ___
53. Square snack with a round hole
55. Paixiao, wot or siku
57. Part of a certain GOAT's sobriquet
58. One way to check out bands
59. Step on it
60. Mic check word

DOWN

1. Cracked
2. Mix format, once
3. Junk drawer contents: Abbr.
4. Asparagus on Broadway, for one
5. Muscle Shoals Rhythm Section, by birth
6. Big bird
7. Chic genre
8. ___ Paul
9. Coats electrochemically
10. Schoolteacher in a 1957 hit, and its 1959 sequel
11. [It's gone!]
12. It may spell trouble for a group of people
13. What raising an index finger to one's lips may mean
14. "I will!"
21. Dispersed
23. Succeed
24. "Vampire on ___" (classic Guided By Voices album)
26. Cervical screenings, for short
27. Carnival conveyance
28. Fail to produce results
30. Handel opera about a sorceress who transforms discarded lovers into rocks and animals
32. Traces
33. Anonymous experimental art band represented by The Cryptic Corporation, with "The"
34. It's a numbers game
36. Dessert whose name means "pick me up" in Italian
39. QB's goofs
43. Butterfly, for one
44. Large spotted rodents
45. Puttered around
46. Knock on
48. "À nous la liberté" filmmaker Clair
50. Swinging London wear
51. "It's ___!"
52. Composer Alban of the Second Viennese School
54. Amt. of vanilla, often
56. Place

(answers on page 120)

SLEEVE CAPTCHA
CAN YOU IDENTIFY THESE NINE CLASSIC ALBUM COVERS?

COMPLETE ME

HOW WELL DO YOU KNOW THE NEW PORNOGRAPHERS' CARL NEWMAN?
FILL IN THIS PARAGRAPH OF BIOGRAPHICAL TRIVIA, PENNED BY THE MUSICIAN HIMSELF.

I learned my first guitar chords when I was _____. They were E, A, and D, which was enough chords

to play _____ by Them and _____ by REM. Then I bought the _____ *Complete Easy Guitar*

songbook, which taught me the rest of the chords. My first band was _____, formed in the city of

_____, solely because we thought we had the dumbest band name and needed a band to go with it. We

had ___ guitar players because that is how many guitarists showed up to our first rehearsal. Our records were

released by the San Francisco label _____. Concurrently I developed a love for the songs of Bacharach

and David and Brian Wilson, which made me form the band _____. That band was signed to the Seattle

label ____ ____ for two records, after which we broke up. Around that time I met ___ _____, who had a

lo-fi project called _____. I thought he was the best songwriter I'd ever met in the local scene. I also met

____ ____, who was the drummer in a local band Meow and had started writing and singing her own songs.

We started the band New Pornographers. The bassist/producer was John Collins; the drummer was ____

_____; and the keyboardist was Kathryn Calder. That band signed to local indie label _____ and we later

signed to the New York City label _____. We became the, no _____, _____ band of all time.

SUBMISSIONS

PENCILHOUSE—We read WIPs and write feedback on 'em, simple as that. FREE submissions monthly, capacity-capped; $6/mo for submit-whenever, cap-free subs. ALWAYS SEEKING VOLUNTEER CRITICS. *Pencilhouse.org*.

ALL ABOARD

LITTLE ENGINES—Issue Nine is out now and includes Kevin Morby, Bob Hicok, Bethany Ball, and Kyle Seibel. Free in print. Zero dollars, straight to your mailbox. You just have to ask: *littleengines.pub*

CHOO CHOO, MOTHERF*CKER—We're a small Risograph press publishing zines and chapbooks with an emphasis on obsession, nostalgia, and states of liminality. Say hi @ *choochoopress. com*.

EARWORMS

INTRODUCING FEELSING—A debut album of post-rock beats, grooves, and atmospheres for listeners and readers of all ages, by DJ Baby Chocolate. To listen to the album and other unique sound worlds, go to *eartrumpetrecordings. bandcamp.com*.

GUTSY RADIO—Seven nights a week of live, webcast, DJ-driven shows from across these United States. 2-hour volunteer slots of music and attitude. Community radio for all. This is not a test. *https:// gutsyradio.org*

FELICITATIONS

HAPPIEST OF BIRTHDAYS to our lover of alternate dimensions, black holes, wild mushrooms, and dynamite. Mr. JB, hope you have the most wonderful day!

WAY TO GO! You did it, Jem! So proud of all your hard work, so happy for you, and so very eager to read your novel soon!

CLASSIFIEDS

Believer Classifieds cost $2 per word. They can be placed by emailing classifieds@thebeliever.net. All submissions subject to editorial approval. No results guaranteed.

OLDER AND WISER? Our precious Willa girl, we can't believe you're already twenty-one. Wishing you the most wonderful day, full of belly rubs, treats, and naps.

MISSED CONNECTIONS

PARALLEL BOOKWORMS—Nancy, I did very much enjoy *Parallel Lives*, and can't believe I hadn't picked it up sooner. I can't say the Victorians had it all figured out, but something about writing back to you here, perhaps one in a sea of missed connections—it makes me wonder. If you'd like to keep discussing, Phyllis Rose or otherwise, let me know through this Classifieds page. Yrs, F.B.

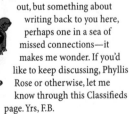

FINDING MY WAY?—Woman with dark hair, working through her Morning Pages at Ciao on Vanderbilt with a Jindo by her side. I'd love to know, if you're open to sharing: do you have a favorite, preferably ergonomic-friendly pen? My metacarpals struggle to get through even one page, though I'm persisting. I hope you might see this, and write back through this Classifieds page. Your fellow artist-in-training, Rafael.

PUBLICATIONS

BEN AFFLECK SPOTTED, WITH DUNKIN' IN HAND—Potentially. Probably. Plausibly. *No Contact Magazine* is open for submissions in short-form Fiction, Non Fiction, Poetry. Just think to yourself: would Ben like this? More at *nocontactmag.com*.

IF I CLOSE MY EYES—New York poet Ben Fama's debut novel, a Hollywood satire about two strangers who begin an affair after surviving a mass shooting at a Kim Kardashian book signing, set for release from new publisher SARKA on Oct. 10, 2023. See *sarkapublishing.com* for more.

AN INCENSE NAMED MAGENTA—Poems about poetry and altered states of consciousness by Peter Patapis, forthcoming Choo Choo Press, Winter 2023.

EAT THE RICH—In a future where rain is reserved for the ultra-rich, the world's only umbrella maker is framed for a high profile murder. C.R. Foster's debut novel *The Rain Artist* is *Succession* meets *The Fifth Element*, with a glorious and gory twist. Find your copy wherever queer lit is sold, or see *moonstruck-books.com* for more.

COST OF PAPER!—An unprintable publication. *costofpaper.com*.

IF YOUR BOOK IS A WEDGE IN A CRACK—Split/Lip Press is the hammer helping you split the wall apart. Use code SLPBELIEVER at splitlippress.com for 25% off your next order of boundary-breaking books and don't miss *SISTER GOLDEN CALF*, an unforgettable road trip story from debut author Colleen Burner.

SERVICES

USF MFA IN WRITING—Fiction, Nonfiction, Poetry, Cross-genre. Small classes, TAships, one-on-one thesis instruction. See *www.usfca.edu/mfa* for more details.

WRITE UNBORING PLAYS—Classes, accountability, and consults for inquisitive, rebellious dramatists. Shake it up. *katetarker.com*

Illustrations by Tomi Um

INTERNATIONAL MUSIC CHARTS

A snapshot of chart-toppers from six different countries.

COMPILED BY BRYCE WOODCOCK, ACCORDING TO 2022 ANNUAL LISTS

MALI

1. "Diarabi Nene Bena" ("Beautiful Woman") by Sidiki Diabaté
2. "Love Guinnée" ("Love Guinea") by Sidiki Diabaté
3. "Barika" ("Gratitude") by Safi Diabaté, Oumou Sangaré
4. "Hamed Dollar" ("Praise of the Dollar") by Mariam Ba Lagaré
5. "Diya" ("Light") by Malakey feat. Sidiki Diabaté
6. "Mama Lah" by Iba One
7. "Atégban" by Imilo Lechanceux feat. Sidiki Diabaté
8. "Dance for Me" by Iba One
9. "Kita Blo" ("Kita Pride") by Prince Diallo
10. "Ni Moko Masa" ("I Love You") by Djinxi B

JAPAN

1. "Zankyosanka" ("Reverberation Song") by Aimer
2. "W/X/Y" by Tani Yuuki
3. "Betelgeuse" by Yuuri
4. "Mixed Nuts" by Official Hige Dandism
5. "Dried Flower" by Yuuri
6. "Cinderella Boy" by Saucy Dog
7. "New Genesis" by Ado
8. "Nandemonaiyo" ("It's OK") by Macaroni Empitsu
9. "Suiheisen" ("Horizon") by Back Number
10. "Ichizu" ("Devoted") by King Gnu

INDIA

1. "Excuses" by Intense, AP Dhillon, Gurinder Gill
2. "Desires" by AP Dhillon, Gurinder Gill
3. "Pasoori" ("Difficulty/Trouble") by Ali Sethi, Shae Gill
4. "Insane" by AP Dhillon, Shinda Kahlon, Gminxr, Gurinder Gill
5. "Ranjha" ("Lover") by B. Praak, Jasleen Royal
6. "Spaceship" by AP Dhillon, Shinda Kahlon, Gminxr
7. "Bijlee Bijlee" ("Lightning") by Harrdy Sandhu
8. "Tere Te" ("Dedication to You") by AP Dhillon, Gurinder Gill
9. "Kesariya" ("Saffron") by Amitabh Bhattacharya, Arijit Singh, Pritam
10. "Doobey" ("Drown") by Lothika, OAFF, Savera, Kausar Munir

CUBA

1. "Bam Bam" by Camila Cabello feat. Ed Sheeran
2. "Ay Mi Dios" ("Oh My God") by IAmChino
3. "Háblame de Miami" ("Talk to Me About Miami") by Gente de Zona, Maffio
4. "Hasta los Dientes" ("To the Teeth") by Camila Cabello, Maria Becerra
5. "Complicado" ("Complicated") by Malú Trevejo feat. Luar La L
6. "El Taxi" by Pitbull feat. Osmani Garcia
7. "Cómo Te Pago" ("How Can I Pay You") by Lenier
8. "La Historia" ("History") by El Taiger
9. "Psychofreak" by Camila Cabello feat. Willow
10. "Si No Vuelves" ("If You Don't Return") by Gente de Zona

INDONESIA

1. "Hati-Hati di Jalan" ("Be Careful Along the Way") by Tulus
2. "Runtuh" ("Collapse") by Feby Putri
3. "Tak Ingin Usai" ("Don't Want It to End") by Keisya Levronka
4. "Sisa Rasa" ("Aftertaste") by Mahalini
5. "Angel Baby" by Troye Sivan
6. "Ghost" by Justin Bieber
7. "Merasa Indah" ("Feel Beautiful") by Tiara Andini
8. "Until I Found You" by Stephen Sanchez
9. "Glimpse of Us" by Joji
10. "Bertahan Terluka" ("Surviving Injury") by Fabio Asher

EGYPT

1. "El Bakht" ("Lucky Cards") by Wegz
2. "Etnaset" ("Forgotten") by MUSliM
3. "Barbary" by Marwan Pablo
4. "Be'oda Ya Belady" ("Come Back, My Country") by Wegz
5. "Aloomek" ("I Blame You") by Marwan Moussa
6. "Mesh Nadman" ("We Don't Regret It") by MUSliM
7. "Akwa Mix" ("Strong Mix") by Wegz, Ahmed Mekky
8. "Ta3ala Adala3ak" ("Come On Let Me Pamper You") by Bahaa Sultan
9. "Hadootet Almany" ("German Story") by Marwan Moussa
10. "Keify Keda" ("This Is How I Feel") by Wegz, Disco Misr

NOTES ON OUR CONTRIBUTORS

Aku Ammah-Tagoe is a writer and interviewer in San Francisco. She has a PhD in English from Stanford University, and her work explores formally innovative art about contemporary life. Aku is making a podcast about the history, artistry, and fan culture of K-pop; follow her progress at aku-at.com or at @akuat on Instagram.

Benjamin Anastas is the author of three novels and a memoir. Other work has appeared in *The New Yorker, Oxford American, Harper's Magazine,* and *The Paris Review*.

Gabriel Bump is from South Shore, Chicago. He is the author of *Everywhere You Don't Belong* and *The New Naturals*.

Alan Chazaro is the author of *This Is Not a Frank Ocean Cover Album* (Black Lawrence Press, 2019), *Piñata Theory* (Black Lawrence Press, 2020), and *Notes from the Eastern Span of the Bay Bridge* (Ghost City Press, 2021). He is a graduate of June Jordan's Poetry for the People program at UC Berkeley and a former Lawrence Ferlinghetti Poetry Fellow at the University of San Francisco. He is proud to have been raised by Mexican immigrants in the Bay Area and is currently a staff writer for KQED Arts and Culture.

Paul Collins is the author of ten books of nonfiction; a newly revised edition of his collection *Banvard's Folly: Thirteen Tales of People Who Didn't Change the World* is now available as an audiobook. He is a professor in the Creative Writing program at Portland State University.

Rob Curran is an Irish writer based in Denton, Texas. His work has appeared in *The Wall Street Journal, The Dallas Morning News, McSweeney's Internet Tendency,* and elsewhere. He is the coauthor, with anthropologist Andrew Nelson, of *Journey Without End: Migration from the Global South Through the Americas*.

Anaïs Duplan is a trans* poet, curator, and artist. He is the author of the book *I NEED MUSIC* (Action Books, 2021); a book of essays, *Blackspace: On the Poetics of an Afrofuture* (Black Ocean, 2020); a full-length poetry collection, *Take This Stallion* (Brooklyn Arts Press, 2016); and a chapbook, *Mount Carmel and the Blood of Parnassus* (Monster House Press, 2017). He is a professor of postcolonial literature at Bennington College and has taught poetry at the New School, Columbia University, and Sarah Lawrence College, among other places.

Megan Fernandes is the author of *The Kingdom and After* (Tightrope Books, 2015) and *Good Boys* (Tin House, 2020). Her third book of poetry, *I Do Everything I'm Told* (Tin House), was published in summer 2023. Her work has been published in *The New Yorker, The American Poetry Review, Ploughshares,* and *Chicago Review,* among other publications. She is an associate professor of English and the writer-in-residence at Lafayette College.

Fernando A. Flores was born in Reynosa, Tamaulipas, Mexico, and is the author of *Valleyesque* and *Tears of the Trufflepig*. He lives in Austin, Texas.

Ricardo Frasso Jaramillo is a poet and writer. His work can be found in *The New York Times, McSweeney's Quarterly, The Rumpus,* and *The Adroit Journal,* among other venues. He currently teaches in the English Department of the Universidad Nacional Autónoma de México, in Mexico City.

Stu Horvath is a writer from New Jersey. He is the founder of Unwinnable, an online outlet for independent cultural criticism. He also manages the @VintageRPG account on Instagram and cohosts the *Vintage RPG* podcast. His book, *Monsters, Aliens, and Holes in the Ground: A Guide to Tabletop Roleplaying Games from D&D to Mothership,* was published by the MIT Press in October 2023.

Emma Ingrisani's writing has appeared in *Full Stop, Post-Trash,* and *The Creative Independent*. She lives in Brooklyn, New York.

Casey Jarman is a writer, illustrator, and *Believer* contributing editor based in Portland, Oregon. He writes (mostly about video-game soundtracks) for Bandcamp.com, and has made animated music videos for Typhoon, Mo Troper, the Shivas, and other friends. *The Guardian* said that his 2016 book, *Death: An Oral History,* would "make you cry in public," and that made him weirdly happy.

Lauren LeBlanc is a writer and editor who has written for *The New York Times Book Review, The Atlantic,* and *Vanity Fair,* among other publications. Born and raised in New Orleans, she now lives in Chapel Hill, North Carolina. She is also a board member of the National Book Critics Circle.

John Lingan's most recent book, *A Song for Everyone: The Story of Creedence Clearwater Revival,* was named a Best Music Book of 2022 by *Variety*. He lives in Maryland.

Melissa Locker is a writer and music podcast impresario in the making. She lives on the internet and runs on coffee. You can follow her at @woolyknickers but not in real life.

Mimi Lok is a writer, editor, oral historian, and narrative strategist. She is the author of *Last of Her Name,* winner of a PEN/Robert W. Bingham Prize and a California Book Award Silver Medal, and is also a Smithsonian Ingenuity Award winner and a National Magazine Award finalist. Mimi is the cofounder of Voice of Witness, an oral history nonprofit that amplifies marginalized voices. She is currently working on a novel and a story collection.

Mike McGonigal lives in Detroit, where he edits the full-color quarterly *Maggot Brain* for Third Man Records & Books. He's compiled multiple reissues of gospel music, including the album *Fire in My Bones,* produces a weekly radio show called '*Buked & Scorned,* and is currently finishing up the gospel-history book *Walk Around Heaven All Day* for Farrar, Straus and Giroux.

Claire Mullen is a producer and editor of audio, texts, and images. She was a fellow with the National Book Critics Circle from 2019-2021. She is currently studying film preservation and archive studies in the Basque Country, Spain.

Niela Orr is a story editor for *The New York Times Magazine,* an editor-at-large of *The Believer,* and a contributing editor of *The Paris Review*. Her writing has appeared in the *London Review of Books, BuzzFeed, The Baffler,* and *McSweeney's Quarterly,* among other publications.

Gray Tolhurst is a writer and a musician. He received his MFA in poetry from San Francisco State University in 2016. He plays in the post-punk band Topographies, who released their debut album, *Ideal Form,* with Funeral Party records in 2020. Their sophomore album, *Interior Spring,* is due in early 2024 from the San Francisco label Dark Entries Records. Gray makes his home in San Francisco with his wife, the artist rel robinson, and their dog, Meatyard.

Ryan H. Walsh is a musician, journalist, and video/collage artist from Boston. His debut book, *Astral Weeks: A Secret History of 1968* (Penguin Press), received rave reviews in *The New Yorker, The Guardian,* and *Rolling Stone,* and was a *New York Times* end-of-year Critics' Pick. His long-running band, Hallelujah the Hills, has toured with acts like the Silver Jews and Titus Andronicus, while releasing seven full-length albums as well as scores of singles, EPs, and experimental works. Their latest album, 2019's *I'm You,* was declared "Album of the Year" by *Glorious Noise* and "a lyrical masterpiece" by *Metro*.

IN THE NEXT ISSUE

Not all contents are guaranteed; replacements will be satisfying

SOLUTIONS TO THIS ISSUE'S GAMES AND PUZZLES

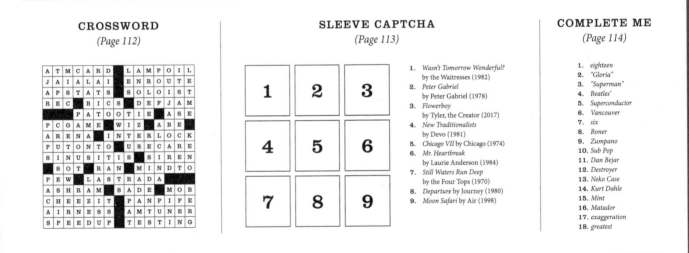

CROSSWORD
(Page 112)

SLEEVE CAPTCHA
(Page 113)

1. *Wasn't Tomorrow Wonderful?* by the Waitresses (1982)
2. *Peter Gabriel* by Peter Gabriel (1978)
3. *Flowerboy* by Tyler, the Creator (2017)
4. *New Traditionalists* by Devo (1981)
5. *Chicago VII* by Chicago (1974)
6. *Mr. Heartbreak* by Laurie Anderson (1984)
7. *Still Waters Run Deep* by the Four Tops (1970)
8. *Departure* by Journey (1980)
9. *Moon Safari* by Air (1998)

COMPLETE ME
(Page 114)

1. *eighteen*
2. *"Gloria"*
3. *"Superman"*
4. *Beatles'*
5. *Superconductor*
6. *Vancouver*
7. *six*
8. *Boner*
9. *Zumpano*
10. *Sub Pop*
11. *Dan Bejar*
12. *Destroyer*
13. *Neko Case*
14. *Kurt Dahle*
15. *Mint*
16. *Matador*
17. *exaggeration*
18. *greatest*

MICROINTERVIEW WITH VICTOR OLADIPO, PART IX

THE BELIEVER: What drew you to Afrobeats as a genre?

VICTOR OLADIPO: I have a deep connection to Afrobeats. I remember when Afrobeats wasn't even played in America. I only heard it at African parties with my family and our friends, on the weekends when my mom would take us. To see how it has evolved, with people doing Ancestry.com to learn about their native backgrounds because of this music—it's crazy. But it's not a shock either. If you step back, Africa is the heart of the world. The way it keeps pushing the culture, the style, the sounds. The world is a better place because of Afrobeats. It's feel-good music. It's a vibe. A lot of people might be intimidated at first because they might not know what's being expressed or explained—but you don't have to understand it to feel it. ✦